phil.

THE SCIENCE AND
ETHICS OF EQUALITY

THE SCIENCE

AND ETHICS OF

EQUALITY

═══

DAVID HAWKINS

═══

BASIC BOOKS, INC., PUBLISHERS

NEW YORK

Library of Congress Cataloging in Publication Data

Hawkins, David, 1913–
   The science and ethics of equality.

   (The John Dewey Society lecture; no. 16)
   Includes index.
   1. Ability. 2. Equality. 3. Teachers,
Professional ethics for. I. Title. II. Series:
The John Dewey Society lectureship series; no. 16.
BF431.H355   171'.2   77-3617
ISBN: 0-465-07237-2

CONTENTS

———

CHAPTER ONE

INTRODUCTION

AS IS TRUE of other deep issues, that of human equality waxes and wanes, appears and disappears like a comet, to return again in some later epoch. Like a comet, it is altered, or should be, by every perihelion passage.

Egalitarian ideas are very old, surely. From the oldest written history they appear, throughout the evolution of urban society, in a form conditioned by the universality of gross and obvious inequalities. Marcus Aurelius the emperor and Epictetus the slave saw themselves, saw all human beings, as equally sparks of the divine Zeus, and as equally condemned to the inequality of their stations and duties. In the Hindu traditions, human beings have an equal, ultimate destiny through the cycles of reincarnation, their differences corresponding to unequal progression along that very long road.

In the Christian tradition Saint Paul announced the equality of all, but he also could imagine it exemplified only in Heaven. In Saint Augustine's lottery of divine grace all persons had, so to speak, equal a priori probability of being chosen to fill the heavenly thrones left empty by the expulsion of Satan and his followers. Since Augustine many revivals have reaffirmed that belief: the meek and lowly have opportunity for salvation as great (if not perhaps greater) as do the aggressive and powerful. Condemned as we all are by Augustinian original sin, we have no basis in wealth or station, or even in manifest moral virtue, to regard ourselves as favored recipients of that grace or election which will tip the scales in our favor.

In both Buddhism and Christianity, at least, this acknowledgment of an ultimate equality is coupled to another basic idea, that of fraternity. Salvation is not only (as in most forms of mysticism) an individual matter; rather those who might be saved or redeemed would choose to stay behind to help the less favored. In these religious contexts (as in Plato's allegory of the cave) there is an acknowledgment that the equivalence or equality of human beings is to be conceived not as they stand in isolation from one another (where their de facto inequality may be manifest enough), but rather as an equivalence that has vitality and meaning within the domain of their interchange and mutual influence. No one is to be judged by any static measure of shortcomings or wrongdoings. This linkage of equality and fraternity is a clue to the analysis of equality as both a descriptive and a moral concept, and I shall return to it.

In the rise of modern secular thought the axiom of equality continued to serve as a standpoint from which the wide spread of social inequality was to be faced as a problem, explained, and either justified or condemned. Thomas Hobbes and René Descartes announced equality as an axiom, Hobbes in political theory and Descartes in the theory of knowledge. J. J. Rousseau and Karl Marx took it as defining the historical starting point: Primitive society is egalitarian. Inequality must be explained historically; it is not an ineluctable fact of nature.

In our own history the founding fathers laid down the principle of equality as an axiom in a sense learned from Euclidean geometry, a common first principle, self-evidently true. They took it as a precondition of rational political existence and of constitutional law. But as a principle, our constitutional equality was not unqualified. It clearly did not exclude economic or other forms of inequality lying outside the sphere of governmental power, as that power was implicitly defined by the rest of the constitution. Still, as the nature of our government and our economic system has evolved, the boundaries of political equality have been repeatedly up for debate, particularly as extensions of egalitarian logic and sentiment have been proposed, going beyond eighteenth-century laissez-faire.

In the face of gross economic differences equality can clearly become an empty principle, as in Anatole France's famous jibe about the magnificent equality of the law, which forbids the rich no less than the poor to sleep under bridges or steal a loaf of bread. In all historical versions of the axiom of equality, indeed, its assertion has a somewhat polemical appearance, belying the claim of obviousness.

The axiom is not asserted as a truism, but as a claim to be set against what is obvious, the generally acknowledged inequality of persons; their moral or intellectual capabilities, their station in society; their power over others. Yet if the axiom is accepted, then it follows that differences in human powers and capacities arise from the uniquely human way in which those powers and capacities are developed through experience. They are learned, evolved through association and practice; and since this practice is essentially social in its context and character, it can properly be called education: a long complex process, starting at birth, by which individuals are or are not "led forth" as members of a society and participants in its culture.

According to modern classical thought, then, the origins of inequality are historical and institutional, and lie in the specific kinds of educational nurture or deprivation which a society affords. Born equal, we can become radically unequal through differences of station and of educational nurture. Institutional inequality perpetuates itself by engendering inequality among persons. It must be an egalitarian commitment, in recognition of this fact, to break the chain that ties each generation to the inequalities of the past.

From the time of Jefferson the principle of equality has been a powerful influence in our debates over education. The older traditions of schooling had clearly been part of the chain of inequality. Formal education was restricted to the few and to the discipline of social class. Indeed the leaders of the movement toward universal public schooling were also typically reformers who criticized the perfunctory, mechanical, and often abusive character of existing school practices. And as we have gone round the clock, through a hundred years of faith in universal education, we have been forced to recognize that the still-new institution of the public schools does not in fact compensate for inequalities of background and status, and may still in many ways accommodate itself to the perpetuation of the very inequalities it was supposed to alleviate.

As we now more fully realize, the preconditions for educational equality cannot by any easy prescription overcome economic and social inequality. Education may redeem,* but education must itself be redeemed. A deep commitment to the study of the educational process—of child development, of the nature of human learning, and of the arts of teaching—is a commitment of the last hundred years, and still a minority one. In our recent history, the study of education—not the institution—was dominated by a powerful and indefatigable character, John Dewey. Dewey had no naive illusions about the separability of educational progress from that of the other institutions of his society. He did not suppose that education of itself would bring about any sudden solution to the problems of American society; on the other hand he did not react against the traditions of enlightenment, as others have done, to see the schools as enslaving institutions which could only function to produce a docile and acquiescent population, accommodated to the insecurities and injustices of our economic system. Dewey saw education as one, but only one, leading influence in the struggle for a more rational and democratic

---

* *Educar es redimir*, a slogan of the ill-fated Spanish Republic.

society. He saw it as worthy of profound intellectual and practical investment.

The issue of equality came round early in the career of John Dewey, when as a young philosopher he joined the ranks of those concerned with social issues. Equality was an issue particularly germane to the then-rising demand for universal public education. The issue of racial equality was one Dewey already knew, but it reached a perihelion in his later life, notably when the Western Christian world's long-standing addiction to antisemitism was raised so brutally to the level of self-consciousness. After Dewey's death, in what may be called the era of Martin Luther King, Jr., that issue has come round again to full visibility, though from century-old origins. Dewey's birth (1859) antedates the abolition of slavery, and in his long life he was well aware that the promise remained unredeemed. I shall return later to Dewey's views. As a secular philosopher he shares a certain insight with the religious philosophies I have mentioned earlier, the linkage of the idea of equality with the idea which Rousseau and the French Revolution restated in political form, that of fraternity.

By the title of this essay I have promised to discuss both the science and the ethics of equality, and after the above sketch as to origins I want to outline briefly how I understand these terms and their relation to the topic of equality. Though the issues are perennial, every period and every crisis have served to focus attention on problems previously glossed over, to bring some illumination, revealing new levels of concern. I do not suppose our time will be an exception to this rule. So the issues will return in some future context; but not stupidly, we hope, as though nothing had been learned.

I have begun by observing the historical fact that in major traditions of concern about the human condition, of concern which puts aside parochial limitations and views its subject in the grandly sweeping viewpoint of religion, or of metaphysics, or of world history, equality has been asserted as an axiom.

In its original meaning an axiom is a proposition so esteemed or deemed worthy of belief that it should be put first in the order of argument. An axiom is not a proposition beyond question in an absolute sense, but it should be the last to be questioned. If an axiom leads to conclusions which seem contrary to fact or which throw doubt on congenial beliefs we should first look more closely at the facts or reexamine our other beliefs. It was an axiom of Euclid's geometry that things equal to the same thing are equal to each other. This example of a logical axiom suggests why it was often said that the truth of an axiom was self-evident. If we use the concept of mathematical equality in clear and familiar ways, the axiom is indeed self-evident, true by virtue of what the term means. If we have asserted that $A = B$ and that $A = C$, but find that $B \neq C$, we are required logically to say that one or both of the assertions were made in error. The axiom itself is not to be questioned.

The proposition that all men are created equal, considered as axiomatic, has obviously a different sort of priority. Some generic beliefs, and this one is an example, have a privileged status not because their denial would be self-contradictory but because they are entwined with so many other beliefs that to deny them is to become rudderless. When such a belief is challenged the characteristic defense is not to adduce specific factual evidence but rather to emphasize how much the challenger stands to lose, intellectually, in throwing it away. In one of the classic statements of English jurisprudence there occurs this summary of such a defense: The memory of man runneth not to the contrary.

The most obvious entwinements of the axiom of equality lie in the domains of ethics and jurisprudence. To weigh the welfare of one person or group over that of another is, without special immediate justification, immoral. To credit the beliefs of one person or tribe or tradition as inherently superior to those of another, except on the basis of special evidence available to all, is unjustifiable. To enter the moral universe of discourse at all is to be committed to set aside egocentric viewpoints, to make judgments so formed that others can examine and criticize them. Inequality, in discussions of distributive justice, can always be criticized, and the defense must always lie in claims of special need or merit on the part of those who benefit. However atypical in practice, equality is a presupposition of public discourse.

But the axiom of equality has its purely factual implications also, implications that we can approach scientifically. A major part of this book is concerned with these scientific questions. The relation between the scientific and the ethical implications of equality is not simple, it is no simpler than the general philosophical question of the relation between the "is" and the "ought." If we identify them too closely, morality becomes meaningless; if we separate them too far apart, it becomes powerless.

There are a number of standard intellectual postures related to this duality of fact and value, and we are all familiar with them. Many persons are morally unwilling or at least publicly unwilling to deny the axiom of equality in its moral implications (Christians, for example), but believe it to be false in fact. Pious pretense is thus sanctified. Others argue that the de facto inequalities among human beings are so conspicuous that the alleged axiom of equality can only be understood as a superstition or a fraud. In the modern revolutionary traditions inequality has been seen as entirely a product of unjust social institutions. In the anarchists' version of this belief the destruction of the state would be followed by a spontaneous reappearance of true equality.

I wish to make use of the ideas of the modern classical philosophers to lay a kind of basic groundwork, a platform for further discussion. They did indeed assert the axiom of equality as a statement of a factual truth about human beings, and they drew from this, together with other "natural laws," many specifically moral and political conclusions. More recent philosophers have given these classical writers a hard time; not because the critics are against equality, but on the general ground that those theories attempted to derive moral principles from purely factual arguments, doing a kind of illegitimate logical glide from the "is" to the "ought." But this kind of criticism often does its own kind of logical glide, from the correct statement that moral judgments cannot be deduced from factual ones, to the false conclusion that these two kinds of judgments are logically unrelated to each other. Factual premises alone are not sufficient for moral conclusions, it is true; but they are remarkably necessary. In particular, any essential inequality among persons, set forth as a claim of fact about their innate talents and capacities, will bear very powerfully upon the purport and meaning of moral and political egalitarianism as a morally tenable position.

I hold the view that the classical writers were not in any serious way guilty of making illicit moral deductions from premises of fact. Their assertion that human beings are born equal, that equality is the "natural" state of affairs, meant first of all that there is no divine sanction for inequality of the sort they protested. More positively, it implied that the important kinds of inequalities were manmade, artificial rather than inevitable. The axiom of equality thus brought the whole discussion of equality and inequality within the sphere of potential human control and thus endowed it with the status of *being* a moral issue.

The immediate and compelling historical background for this new turn in political thought lay, undoubtedly, in the growing religious and political disturbances of Europe during, and after, the period we call the Renaissance, which in its socioeconomic aspect can also be called the period of the decadence of feudalism. What was left to conceive of as the unit of social grouping and control was the human individual abstracted from any secure status as lord, freeholder, serf, merchant, or priest. But this conception did not appear as something "abstract"; it had the clothing of an immediate reality. I think of the Levellers of England, and of a voice protesting in Cromwell's Parliament: "The poorest He in England hath a life to live, no less than the richest He."

After three of the most extraordinary centuries in human history, our own practical concerns about equality have a somewhat different character, already suggested above. Our intellectual outlook has so altered since Darwin and Lewis Henry Morgan, moreover, that if we can still learn from the classics it must be by translating them to a new context and subjecting them to new tests. That is something which I propose to do, to sketch at least, in the following chapter. The argument leads to a sort of first approximation view of innate human differences, with respect to which I shall argue that no one today can reasonably *not* be egalitarian. What this means is that innate human differences will not provide explanations for any central phenomena of anthropology, for any of the major unevenness of human history, or important inequalities of human status; they will not provide valid factual support for invidious distinctions, of a kind we have long known, in morals, politics, or the provision of care and education for the young.

Against the background of this conclusion I shall then be prepared in chapters three and four to analyze a range of real human differences which lie within the bounds thus established, but which are to be taken account of in any good second approximation picture of human affairs, and which are—as I shall hold—of major, though badly neglected, importance in the theory and practice of education. In chapter five I shall try to state an ethically and scientifically valid egalitarian position which is, at the same time, a challenge to further research and practical educational effort.

CHAPTER TWO

BIOLOGICAL EQUALITY—
A FIRST
APPROXIMATION

———

IN RECENT DEBATE over the issue of equality and in-equality there has been a revival and revamping of the old nature-nurture controversy, and that is a subject I shall discuss at some length in the next chapter. Much of this controversy has taken place in a sort of dual context which I believe confuses the debate and infects it with error. One context is that of academic research; the other is that of social policy. These two arenas cannot and should not be isolated from each other, yet statements and arguments intended for one audience have a way of acquiring a quite altered freight of implications when intercepted by the other.

Nevertheless this intersection of contexts brings opportunity with it, the opportunity to develop a framework of ideas adequate to the many aspects of the subject. Some of these, important both for scientific purposes and relevant, at the same time, to questions of social and education policy, have not been defined at all or have been lost sight of—either in the heat of public debate or in the coolness of academic environments where self-limiting intellectual habits and research methods may have gone too long unchallenged. In most recent discussions one finds relatively little attention given to the history of earlier debate—spanning indeed the last fifty years—as though nothing fresh could be relearned from it.* This history is important not only because of its obvious moral and political implications, but also in the interest of scientific probity and progress.

As a first step I intend to go back still further to the time of those seventeenth- and eighteenth-century philosophers who first laid down the modern egalitarian axiom. I could, of course, go even further back than Rousseau or Descartes or Hobbes, to Aristotle and Plato. It is at least worth a reminder that both those ancient philosophers took for granted a natural biological inequality not only with respect to sex but also with respect to political and economic status. "Some men," said Aristotle, "are born to be slaves."

Such views, one need hardly say, are native to aristocratic societies and, in the life of such societies, powerfully self-confirming. Spartan masters were the natural superiors of their Helot serfs, Greeks were naturally superior to Barbarians, men were obviously superior to women. It is true that Plato moved far enough from conventional views to

---

* This early history is reviewed in Otto Klineberg, *Race Differences* (New York: Harper & Bros., 1935). *See also*, his *Race and Psychology* (Paris: UNESCO, 1951).

question the lowly status of Athenian women. He also came close enough to modern truisms of genetics to suggest that Iron or Silver children could be born to Golden parents, and vice versa. In the *Republic* he therefore asks for something like a Stanford-Binet or Bellevue-Wechsler intelligence test—a request that took two thousand years to satisfy.

Let me begin, more seriously, with the theoretical structure erected by Thomas Hobbes. Hobbes is a very important figure in modern social philosophy. He had few followers, it is true. But fortunate is the philosopher known by such critics! Subsequent political and ethical theory has been so laden with refutations of Hobbes that one must acknowledge him as the very father of modern political theory—of the whole enterprise carried on by Locke, Rousseau, Hegel, Marx, and, I may add, John Dewey.*

Hobbes' adoption of the axiom of human equality is of special interest for my purposes because on his part this cannot be regarded as a wishful or ideological move, but directs us to reflect upon the logical preconditions of any adequate social theory. Hobbes was as firm a critic of democracy as any rational man could be, and his ideal government was an absolute monarchy. But such views do not distinguish him from others who took the side of the pre-revolutionary monarchy, nor explain his intellectual power and influence. His thought goes deeper, and his axiom of equality is basic to it.

Let me put it this way: Hobbes' approach to the exami-

---

* John Dewey, *The Public and Its Problems* (Chicago: Gateway Books, 1946).

nation of human society is not that of one bent on empirical, historical description in common-sense terms, but rather more like that of a theoretical physicist. Given certain laws describing the interactions within the elements of a system, one then derives the particular states, or in modern jargon "eigenvalues" of the system, for which these laws are satisfied. Newton was to do the same kind of analysis, several decades later, in showing that his laws of motion and of gravitation led to a family of particular solutions which included Kepler's already formulated descriptions of the planetary orbits. A predecessor of Newton but a follower of Galileo and Harvey, Hobbes' imagination was fired by the power of the new mechanicl science.

Hobbes' laws are quite simple. Human beings are equal, they are rational, and by nature they assign the highest priority to their individual self-preservation. Given these "laws" (none particularly original), Hobbes deduces two possible eigenvalues, states of human existence. One is his famous "war of each against all," the other is civil society under a sovereign who has the power of life or death over all others.

The possibility of Leviathan, of civil society as a man-made solution of the problem of human coexistence, arises from the same axioms as the state of war. One of Hobbes' theorems is that all men, as equal, rational, and committed to self-preservation, will "endeavor peace." War destroys for most, and sooner or later for all, the very means of life and security which lead them, under conditions of scarcity and anarchy, to inevitable collision with each other. The endeavor for peace cannot, however, be achieved except through the institution of a state power which will grant security to all individuals and will insure to them the benefits of their cooperation.

It is unfortunate that Hobbes did not have the advantage of association with a famous twentieth-century mathematician, John von Neumann, who with his collaborator Otto Morgenstern developed the mathematical theory of games.* It is also unfortunate that, so far as I know, those authors paid no attention to Hobbes, who with less mathematical sophistication anticipated both their style of thought and some of their conclusions.

The analysis of games of strategy reveals a remarkable gap in the logic of self-interest. In games of more than two players, or in games where the gain to one player is not necessarily a loss to the others, the choice among various modes of competition or cooperation becomes itself a decisive aspect of the play. There is in general no best strategy for individual players unless a "standard of behavior" dominates their moves and countermoves, a tacit or explicit acceptance of some one way of playing the game which the rules themselves do not require. Thus, for example, two players may make a compact to exploit a third by letting him have less than his cooperative share. Any counteroffer the exploited player may make to one of the exploiters can be met by the other exploiter, so long as the exploiters share their gains. Thus, in general there will be many divisions of gain which are all "solutions" of many-person games, and the choice among these solutions is in some sense or other a

---

* John von Neumann and Otto Morgenstern, *Theory of Games and Economic Behavior* (New York: John Wiley & Sons, 3rd ed., paper, 1964).

social decision, not a decision based solely on the self-interest of the individual players. If some effective set of players elect such a solution, no consideration of rational self-interest will be able to move them from it to another solution. Considerations of utility and bargaining power determine a set of possible outcomes of the game which are all potentially, and equally, solutions. The choice among these is logically indeterminate except as an effective set of players forms around and adopts some one of them. Once such a standard of behavior is adopted in this way it cannot be dominated by any other solution.

The general moral to be derived from game theory is that individualistic utilitarianism of itself does not lead to any single determinate solution, but to an incommensurable array of solutions. The choice among these requires some other logical and philosophical basis, some form of Hobbesian compact. Those who have criticized Hobbes for introducing this notion have been wrong, I think, in missing the subtlety of his analysis. His social contract represents—mathematically—an essential characteristic of stable human society.

I should add that although the inventors of game theory seemed to pay no attention to their illustrious predecessor, their own motivation was not lacking in breadth. John von Neumann once explained, in private conversation, that he hoped to show, by formal analogy, how under altered standards of behavior the game of capitalism could be brought to compete with that of socialism in providing distribution standards at least as fair and equitable as those which socialism promised.

To continue with Hobbes: Under his contract all individuals agree with each other to surrender their power to a sovereign or government, a person or body of persons who himself or themselves remain outside the contract. The sovereign will find it to his advantage to grant back all those powers which do not threaten domestic tranquility and industry, and will rule in accordance with a system of civil law which gives his subjects least reason to regret the contract. In particular, the sovereign will guarantee to each the continued enjoyment of his life and property, depriving him of these only as he may endanger the lives and properties of others. Unless men were equal, they would not have entered the contract. They must therefore be afforded equal protection under the law. Unless they were rational, they would not have seen the advantage of the contract or have entered it willingly; being rational, they have bound themselves to forego war against fellow citizens, and have accepted the possibility of punishment for transgression. Being committed by nature to their own self-preservation, they accept a curtailment of those amoral liberties of action against each other which they would, in any case, have recourse to only because of the anarchy and insecurity of the state of nature.

And here again is the conceptual discontinuity of which I spoke. Starting from axioms which are by intent entirely *descriptive* of human nature, they lead to a social solution, artificial or man-made in character, which in turn mirrors those axioms in a body of *prescriptive* law. The sovereign will undertake to treat all persons as equal, because in fact they are; will govern rationally, because that is to his own advantage; will protect his subjects against threats to life and liberty, because their consent cannot be otherwise relied upon. If the sovereign is not in any way bound by the contract, he is on the other hand motivated to benefit by it. Others do not threaten him so long as he enforces its terms.

Hobbes' justification of the state of civil society is totally unhistorical in character, as is the contract which is its pivotal step. In the light of history, his solution is only a mathematical one, that is to say a solution the main virtue of which is that it helps *define* the problem it purports to solve.

My own concern with Hobbes, here, is twofold. The first is to underline the use he makes of the axiom of equality. The second, which I shall come back to, is that cluster or system of distinctively human traits associated with the concept, which Hobbes developed in his own way from his reading of Aristotle, of man as a rational animal.

Both in Hobbes' discussion of the meaning of equality, and in the use his theory requires of it, a certain domain of relations is implicitly defined with respect to which we are all "equal." Hobbes cheerfully grants minor differences among men in native endowment: physical strength and quickness of wit, for example. But such inequalities as exist are minor, they lead to no social behavior significantly different from what would be implied by an assumption of strict equality. If human beings were basically unequal, in matters of intelligence and competence, then natural rulers would always rule as a matter of course, and there would be no problem of politics. The turbulent history of civil societies would simply never have been possible. In the face of a firm biological inequality among us no one would doubt the legitimacy of his natural rulers any more than the bees in the hive could doubt the legitimacy of their natural egg-layer, the queen.

Hobbes' self-appointed task was to explain and justify the existence of the state, with its assumption of the power of life and death by some men over others. For him the basis of this justification lay in the contrast between civil society and that state of nature which would prevail in its absence. But the state of nature, the hypothetical condition in which all men found themselves in destructive competition with each other, was likewise only conceivable among equals. Without essential equality there could be no competitive and violent state of nature, no natural law, no social contract to imply a government by binding consent, no civil society rooted in that law and that consent—no *problem* of politics. But there *is* a problem, as all of what Hegel later called the slaughter-bench of history testifies. If there are natural rulers among us, the fact is well concealed. It was vividly a problem of Hobbes' own age of war and civil war, as it is of ours.

Others of Hobbes' age and persuasion could and did take the easy way out, claiming this or that source of divine right, supernatural if not natural legitimacy. Unfortunately, the bases of all such claims have always been obscure and occult, lacking evidence among those wishing to doubt. Hobbes wiped the slate clean, and from then on no political theory has been able to pass muster which did not reckon with the power of Hobbes' central position. The axiom of equality is an axiom necessary to establish the relevance to the real world of *any* political theory. So far as I know no major political thinker has ever seriously tampered with it since, though there is frequent gnawing at the edges.

What Hobbes himself made of his starting point is another matter, and there of course we have a long and fascinating sequel—of Locke and Rousseau, Jefferson and Madison, Hegel and Marx. To which it is entirely appropriate to add the name of John Dewey, whose *The Public and Its Problems* is an elegant reconstruction of classical democratic thought faced with the problems of our own era.

But what does equality itself mean? To say that all men are born equal is to say on Hobbes' account that purely biological, purely "natural," explanations of human hierarchies and exploitations will be disallowed. It is not to deny de facto inequalities, for example, but only to deny that these lie somehow in the nature of things, beyond any possible human nurture, remedy, or responsibility. This is implied in the very title of Rousseau's second discourse, "On the Origins of Inequality". These origins for Rousseau are economic and political inequalities, are human inventions or expedients. Inequality is not nature, but "second" nature, history. Winstanley had said the same thing, and Locke echoed it. You find it in Madison and Jefferson, and for Europe of the nineteenth century, in Hegel and Marx.

In and through this modern intellectual history the central theme of the instability of civilized society has gradually widened from its origins—inquiry concerning the legitimacy of government—to a many-sided investigation of the evolution of human societies and of human culture. From the time of Hobbes the idea of equality has been important in three ways. First, as with Hobbes, it has been central to the recognition that the organization of society has evolved through the conscious actions and inventions of men and is not biologically predetermined, as are the societies of other social animals. Second, as with Rousseau and Marx, the inequalities to which that cultural evolution has ceaselessly given rise are seen not as the "natural" expressions of biological differentiation or inequality, but are conditions for the existence and relative stability of the institutions of work and property under changing historical conditions. Third, as with all the democratic theorists who follow in the turbulent wake of Hobbes, the possibility of a good society has been linked inseparably to the principle of government by consent among equals.

But all of this defines, as I have said, only an overall, first-approximation notion in equality. In our traditions there are countercurrents of belief which seem to threaten it, implicit qualifications which bear closer examination.

Indeed the unselfconscious belief in the natural—biological—superiority of some classes or races, held by their members, is an old and familiar story, one about which we in the United States have special, though by no means unique, reason for concern. The ancestors of present-day Euro-Americans brought it with them, inseparable from the mood of occupation and conquest. And as I said in connection with the views of Aristotle, it tends to be powerfully self-confirming. Perhaps these alleged inequalities would not always be claimed to rank large enough to threaten my first approximation. In the circle of Charles Darwin, Francis Galton, and T. H. Huxley, such inequalities were at any rate taken as obvious. Galton's studies were thought to give scientific support to the belief that "genius" tends to be hereditary. It is not a central matter in Darwin's writing, but he can be found saying that

The variability or diversity of the mental faculties in men of the same race, not to mention the greater differences between men of distinct races, is so notorious that not a word need here be said.*

Or again,

Looking at the distant future, I do not think that the Rev. Mr. Zincke takes an exaggerated view when he says: All other series of events—as that which resulted in the culture of mind in Greece, and that which resulted in the empire of Rome—only appear to have purpose and value when viewed in connection with, or rather as subsidiary to . . . the great stream of Anglo-Saxon migrations to the west."†

But there is perhaps no more characteristic statement than that of T. H. Huxley, who after a grudging expression of his political acquiescence to Lincoln's Emancipation Proclamation goes on to say,

But even those who are most thoroughly convinced that the doom [of slavery] is just, must see good grounds for repudiating half of the arguments which have been employed by the winning side; and for doubting whether its ultimate results will embody the hopes of the victors, though they may more than realize the fears of the vanquished. It may be quite true that some negroes are better than some white men; but no rational

* *The Origin of Species* and *The Descent of Man*, Modern Library edition, (New York), p. 414.
† Ibid., p. 508.

man, cognizant of the facts, believes that the average negro is the equal, still less the superior, of the average white man.*

In all of these abundant writings by nineteenth-century men of science, some of which I could not today quote without being taken as bent upon a sort of retroactive character assassination, one finds the self-revealing unguardedness of attitude, over and above any facts asserted, which is the telltale—the "we" which presupposes a white audience, Darwin's "notorious," Huxley's "rational man," and all that sort of usage.

A very honorable exception is Darwin's coauthor of evolutionary theory, A. R. Wallace, who also, with un-Victorian temerity, believed in the intellectual equality of men and women.

I have here illustrated the parochialism of Europe in Darwin's era in order to contrast it with the vast new historical perspectives his era ushered in, and which today make that parochialism itself seem remote from the real world.

Since the time of Hobbes and Rousseau, since the time of those grand declarations of equality which belonged to the intellectual atmosphere surrounding the American and French Revolutions, a wholly new intellectual perspective has developed, deeply influenced by the Darwinian era but having its own independent factual basis. The seventeenth- and eighteenth-century philosophers set a problem but they lacked the necessary historical knowledge and perspective

* *Science and Education* (New York: D. Appleton and Co., 1897), from "Black and White," p. 66.

to deal with it. Hegel at the beginning of the nineteenth century still lacked it, in spite of his grand synthetic sweep. The history he knew, with all his erudition, was cast in a mold not unlike that of the Rev. Mr. Zincke (quoted above by Darwin), replacing "Anglo-Saxon" by "German." Yet like Rousseau before him and Marx after him, Hegel traced the origins of government to the accumulation of property and the preservation of economic inequality. Speaking of the United States of his day, he made the characteristically haughty statement that the young United States was still in too egalitarian a condition to have become a state in the proper sense.

Even Marx remained Europe-centered in his basic thinking. His scheme of stages was abstracted from the history of ancient, medieval, and modern Europe. He and Frederick Engels knew or suspected that India and China did not fit this pattern, and even speculated on the possibility that oriental societies had somehow evolved within the framework of primitive communism rather than generating the dialectic of slave society. Working in the age of Darwin and of Morgan, they had just the outline of a larger view of human history, to which Engels' *Origins of the Family, Private Property and the State* was itself an important early contribution.

Today almost a hundred years later we have the broad outlines well established. Ethnology conspires with our own recent history to weaken the parochialism of Europe and America, while the results of a hundred years of archeology and paleontology have given us approximately the right time scale and geographic spread. What emerges is a picture of a major and very rapid evolutionary change, one which has transformed the whole character of our planet. Beginnings are relative (and still obscure), but if we allow twenty million years for the biological evolution of the higher primates in general, the major cultural evolution of man has taken place within the last hundred thousand, for some purposes much less. In terms of planetary impact the cultural evolution of man represents an acceleration, by a factor of about a thousand, of any purely biological evolution we know about from the rock record or, from our present-day knowledge of the mechanisms of evolution, can plausibly conceive. This rough time ratio of a thousand to one is essential to the rest of my argument, and defines the spirit in which one can say that changes in human existence brought about by cultural evolution should in the first approximation be thought of as taking place against an *unchanging* genetic background within the human species. Infants from twenty thousand years ago, transported by magic to our maternity wards, would occasion no surprises, nor would their subsequent careers, suitably adopted into the stream of our modern lives. Fifteen or twenty thousand years ago—only 800 generations—*all* of our ancestors were living the lives of hunters and gatherers, in small bands thinly scattered. Occasionally there were larger populations, as in the rich zones below the retreating glaciers. Fire they had, from some far remoter and conceivably prehuman ancestry. Their simple stone tools and weapons we know about, as we do some of their pictograms and paintings. Their language is pure conjecture, but comparative anatomy and physiology require for its evolution a long time scale, a million years in which aptitude and invention, biological and early cultural change, went hand in hand though at the pace of the former.

In any such perspective, viewing the cultural evolution of those last twenty thousand years, it is clear that man— genetically unchanging in a very good first approximation —is in his nature a radically plastic, self-modifying crea- ture. In him biological evolution has superseded itself by producing the great unfilled brain of the human infant, who from birth enters the stream of human life, early assimilates the structures and skills of articulate communication, and becomes in turn a bearer and potential modifier of the cul- ture.

Genetic diversity there surely is, and if equality were to mean genetic identity then no persons would be equal, identical twins aside. Comparison suggests, indeed, that we are more polytypic than most mammalian species. In our biological history we have spread over the globe and lived long enough in relative isolation to develop the obvious genetic frequency patterns we associate with race, along with others less obvious, such as blood groups, etc.

Yet all of this genetic variety is clearly to be placed under the heading, "Second Approximation." What I am saying is obvious, but to pass by it in silence is to cause mischief. Genetic and embryological abnormality and nur- tural insult aside, all men are equally members of their own unique species and are possessed of its universal species- characteristic attributes: above all that plasticity of be- havior, and enormous capacity for the assimilation of ex- tragenetic information; that intersubjective communication link which Hegel called public consciousness; that ability equally to build new models of the universe or to construct new plans of behavior and new social institutions.

When we look so at the human situation we see the profound point in the title of Gordon Childe's classic summary of modern anthropology, *Man Makes Himself*.* The story of cultural evolution is that of a group of biological attributes which other mammals possess in more rudimentary fashion, but which in man have finally broken free of biological constraints and lead a life, an evolution, of their own. Only with us does tool-using aim at producing new tools, or knowledge-using aim toward acquiring new knowledge. And only with us does behavior get transformed into conduct, the central and mysterious artifact of human self-consciousness. In Darwin's day the theologians mostly thought that the uniqueness of man was being minimized by his discoveries, which indeed contradicted the fine old stories which sought to enfranchise that uniqueness. Yet what emerges today, in Darwin's tradition, only underlines the remarkable transformation which we learned about, in childhood, through the story of the Garden of Eden.

In pursuing further the subject of human equality, in the following chapter, I wish to keep in reserve the first-approximation argument suggested in this one. This argument has two sides, mutually supportive. The first is a general declaration, supported by massive qualitative evidence, of the first-order irrelevance of any purely biological gradations or rankings among human individuals, groups, or races, for

* V. Gordon Childe, *Man Makes Himself* (London: New American Library, 1951).

explaining obvious inequalities among us—inequalities not only with respect to social and economic status but also with respect to what we call ability, talent, achievement. The plasticity of the human organism, the "tunability" of the individual nervous system during its long developmental history, outweighs all else. Our genetic differences are grossly insufficient to explain our human diversity.

The other side of the argument is that though our individual and racial biological differences are real, they are not only not sufficient to explain our diversity, they are also not necessary to explain it. Purely biological characteristics, "phenotypes," are in the first approximation determined by the genetic makeup of our cells, our "genotypes." The most humanly important differences are not, for the most part, of that kind, they are not biological, but *cultural*, "phenotypes." Even on the simplifying hypothesis of absolute genetic identity, allowing sexual difference only its basic reproductive importance, our differentiation and diversity could still be fully described in terms of the historical unevenness of cultural evolution, the social stratifications of purely economic and political origin, and the accidental diversity of cultures and of individual lives.

In none of this argument about the origins and nature of human inequality have I committed myself to the view, implicit in much of twentieth-century anthropology, that man the biological animal is mere clay to be shaped by the forces of cultural evolution. It is understandable that anthropology, in breaking away from the parochialism I have alluded to, should have reacted by developing the intellectual posture of cultural determinism, which puts us all on an equal footing biologically. But clay does not shape itself. Human inventiveness is chief among the forces of cultural evolution. Man is the product, but also the producer, the inventor, of all those diverse experiments in ways of life and thought. He would not be the producer except as endowed biologically with a well-defined system of attributes unique in the animal kingdom, a human nature. This nature, though evolved biologically along with and surrounded by the early evolution of culture, is essentially independent of the cultural variety which anthropologists have celebrated. Imprinted on each example of that variety is, so to speak, a common legend: *Homo me fieri fecit*—Man caused me to be made.*

The view I am trying to develop in this essay thus has definite nativistic implications. Human beings are born with a whole range of capacities and potentialities which begin to manifest themselves from birth. These are, indeed, "culture free." But it is not easy to improve on commonsense knowledge in such matters. Since the attributes that interest us are precisely those which are distinctively human, they can hardly manifest themselves except in a fully human context, culture-bound rather than culture-free. We interpret a baby's first gropings and gurglings in the light of what they later will develop into; and the more that behavior becomes refined and elaborated, the more we must recognize in it a source and meaning which is not *biologically* native to the infant. The "how" of this early learning

---

* I borrow the legend from that printed on the flowsheets of the first printed books of England, those of William Caxton, translator and printer: *Caxton me fieri fecit.*

is native endowment; the "what" that we observe is not. But the "what" and the "how" begin immediately to interact.

The male canary chick begins, at a certain stage, to emit a peculiarly tuneless warble. This song evolves slowly into the brilliant song of the adult male, and it does so by the assimilation of what the young bird takes in—the songs of other males, the typewriter, the telephone ringing, the piano, the radio. The beginning seems inborn, its style a characteristic of this species of finch. The final polished repertoire still has a distinctive canary style, but it is a highly individual product. Are we human beings basically different? Is not much of our behavior determined by our genetic makeup?

My general answer, which will be elaborated in the following chapters, is that the range of adaptations of our instinctual equipment as human beings is so much greater than that of the canary, or even the chimpanzee, that the very terms in which we describe human behavior are of a different logical type from those of biology. To map a human instinct—a biologically native behavior tendency—in terms of all its possible mature manifestations, as modified by learning and choice, is an interesting possibility. Rather than argue the difficulty of such a task, let us pretend that it can be done. But then we notice that the reversed mapping —that of any humanly significant type of behavior in terms of its innate origins—is equally diffuse and multiple. Again, let us pretend that this investigation can be carried out. What knowledge will we have gained relative to human virtues, vices, limitations or potentialities? Not a great deal, I think, not much more than by pretending to have done all this elaborate research. The thought experiment alone will surely tell us one thing: that we cannot simply start with some standard phenomenon of human behavior and find for it a one-to-one correspondence with some corresponding genetic complexion.

Consider the category of "aggression." Thanks to the work of the animal ethologists a great deal has been learned about the manifestations, origins, and releasers of aggressive animal behavior and its linkages with territoriality, courtship, and protection of the young. In all of this we surely find counterparts in human behavior. But what is not explained in this way is the very diversity of human behavior. The lamentable and no longer tenable institution of warfare is surely a massive manifestation of aggressive impulses, as well as of many others. Is this institution explained by man's biological inheritance? The very same inheritance can equally explain the marches of such contrasting figures as General Sherman and Mahatma Gandhi —both were highly aggressive! To "fight for what you believe in", whether destructively or creatively, simply has no counterpart in the domain of animal aggression. We thus get an uneasy sense when we realize that to explain our bloody human career in terms of prerational biological compulsions is inevitably also to justify that career, i.e. to declare it inevitable, to take a shortcut which massively ignores the domains of morals, of politics, of education, and of investigations in those areas that minister to the fruitfulness of possible new modes of character and of social existence. Aggression in the animal domain is seldom to be equated with violence; much more often it reflects the need to maintain organization and leadership. Human violence is a quite special phenomenon, more like a product of our distinctive capacities than one which persists, in spite of these capacities, from some prehuman biological past.

Purely biological explanations of specific modes of human behavior suffer from the same fallacious bent as do explanations from popular Freudianism: if the behavior had been different, the explanation would have worked just as well. It is a fallacy of retrospective description, of theoretical claims too loosely defined to be testable by good evidence. The human characteristics I am concerned with in this book are admittedly the most plastic; the most influenced by childrearing, by education, by the life in which alone they can manifest themselves, by all those remarkable synthetic developments which transform organisms into persons and lives into biographies. For all of this the human modification of mammalian genetics is profoundly necessary as ground plan, and profoundly insufficient as explanation.

To summarize: In the first approximation, the domain of relationships across which human beings are equal is that of their membership in a single well-defined species unique in its capacity for education and invention. If our genotypic inheritance were randomly shuffled, at birth, the world would continue on its way (with some surface differences) unaffected in its basic problems and achievements, hopes, and frustrations.

But what is denied at this level must perhaps be readmitted at another. For we are genetically diverse, perhaps more so than most mammalian species. What is to be denied at the first level of approximation, in the interest of a simple theory adequate for major perspectives, may have to be qualified for other and still important purposes.

CHAPTER THREE

NATURE AND NURTURE— INTERACTION

EVERYTHING I have said so far about the axiom of equality is said, to repeat, in the scientific spirit of first and main approximation. Our distinctively human characteristics—the particular language we speak, the clothes we wear, the thoughts we generate, the knowledge we have assimilated, the skills we learn for using tools or logic, for making sonnets or sonatas—these characteristics are essentially nonbiological. If genotype determines phenotype, even in part, then these traits are "nonphenotypic." They grow and diversify by our minds' variations and selections from an evolving pool. This pool is not the gene pool, it is a pool of patterns of thought and conduct. Our biology makes us apt for culture but does not explain culture's evolution or content.

At this point and in this connection, however, I must

refer to a long history of studies relating to statistical associations found between biological ancestry and human abilities. As I have already indicated, belief in the predominantly hereditary character of intelligence and other socially admirable traits was endemic in nineteenth-century Europe and America, and still largely is in the twentieth. It was strongly associated, even among the benign and gentle, with that expansionist commitment which we in America were once taught as our manifest destiny. Such a criticism implies that this claim of self-superiority is false. But that must be a matter of evidence. Indeed the evidence for inequality once seemed to some, in Darwin's word, "incontestable." Out of Western Europe evolved mercantile and industrial technology, science, the high arts of that world, a powerful middle class, political democracy, and worldwide imperialism. Where else in history could that record be equaled?

It was in such an atmosphere that Francis Galton, Darwin's first cousin and a pioneer anthropologist, carried on extensive genealogical studies of "genius," and showed in particular that high talent ran strong in families. Galton was one of the founders of modern statistical theory, and was one of the first to direct attention to the statistical study of biological populations. Galton was also one of the founders of the positive eugenics movement, advocating "improvement of the race" by selective mating. In correlating the characteristics of near relatives (he invented the coefficient of correlation) Galton failed to distinguish hereditary from nonhereditary aspects of that correlation, taking it merely as a measure of genetic influence. This kind of gross error has only been partially corrected in the later development of statistical theory and the theory of polygenic heredity, to which I shall turn next.

In almost all the older and newer population studies of the genetic variability of human traits, especially of "intelligence," there is an assumption which can be a source of error more subtle than Galton's. Having recognized that the traits under investigation originate partly from genetic and partly from nongenetic ("environmental") causes, it is then assumed that the effects of "nature" and of "nurture" are *additive*. This assumption can be traced, I believe, to a time when genetic mechanisms and developmental processes were less well understood than now. Sometimes the interaction of genetic and nongenetic factors may be expressed in this way, but typically it cannot. Such assumptions of additivity are open to scientific investigation, but in the literature I shall discuss they are very often assumed with little or no investigation. Indeed the sort of investigation required may turn out to be quite different from what demographic statistics can readily provide.

In order to illustrate the nature of the relationship between the genetic constitution of living things and the environment in which they develop, I would like to use some particularly simple examples in which such things are quite well understood, namely, from the world of bacteria. Even in such forms of life the genetic code is a storehouse of many distinct chemical recipes, or genes, each of which can influence the flow of chemical activity in the cell to produce molecules of the sort it specifies. These catalytic molecules, by their specific character and abundance, in turn direct the cell chemistry to do all the many jobs, in sequence, of the metabolism of the cell, including its final division into two daughter cells. The two-way-ness of this sequential relationship between the genes and the life of the cell is to be underlined. A gene responsible for catalyzing the production of an enzyme, itself a catalyst of the cell's chemical traffic flow, is active in some phases of the cell life and inactive in others; in one way or another it is turned "on" or "off" and perhaps quantitatively regulated, by the intracellular environment, which in turn is engaged in constant interaction with the environment outside the cell.

The genes are thus not a sort of pattern or prototype of the "completed" organism, as preformationist language would imply, but are "homeorhetic" regulators in the development, step by step, of the cell's structure and its thermodynamic landscape, each stage making accessible the next. The purposiveness of cellular development does not aim at a "final product" (there is no such thing) but only at the next step, step by step.

Now let us back off to a simpler and more external way of looking at the lives of bacterial cells. Their nutritional requirements are generally not too complicated, and it is possible to specify these completely, listing chemical species and their concentrations. Some needed molecules cannot be manufactured by the cells and must be present in the nutrient as raw materials or bearers of free energy. Others, in sufficient concentrations, will destroy the cells or at least inhibit their growth.

But bacteria are, as we have come to know, notoriously adaptable. Mutations are constantly occurring at a rate which is very low per bacterium, but still very frequent in the enormous populations that bacteria generate. These mutations are accidental rearrangements of the molecules which constitute the genetic recipes. Many of these mutations simply render the gene inactive, but others give rise to variant recipes, alleles. Just as there can exist an enormous variety of somewhat different cooking recipes for what may be still called a cheesecake, so there may exist a very large genetic pool of varieties within what may still be given the name of a single bacterial species. At a given moment some of these varieties may be present in large numbers, while many others will be rare. Some will disappear altogether, while others are being generated through mutation. The descendants of a single bacterium will be genetically identical, however, at least until populations have grown large enough to exhibit mutations within them. By selection one can therefore isolate pure varieties and investigate them separately. For some varieties there will be measurable nutritional differences: some will be adapted to lesser amounts of this or that nutrient, some will need specific food substances which others do not; the growth of some will be inhibited by specific agents which others are relatively unaffected by.

Given these general circumstances, I would like to suggest a series of thought experiments to illustrate the "nature-nurture" relationships. Let us take growth-rate, the average frequency of cell divisions per unit time, as the phenotypic characteristic to be observed, and see how this depends, jointly, on genetic makeup and nutrition.

Imagine, first, a standardized soup in which all varieties

will grow, but in general at different rates. If we now vary the concentration of some generally necessary molecular species (or some generally effective toxin), it can happen that all growth rates are increased or decreased in the same proportion. In that case we can speak of the combined effect of heredity and environment as additive, *relative to the given genetic variety and the given range of environmental differences*. The following table of hypothetical growth rates will illustrate the pure case:

TABLE 1

Purely additive relationship between Heredity and Environment.

$$R = 8H + 4E + 36.$$

	E_1	E_2	E_3	E_4	Average
H_1	48	52	56	60	54
H_2	56	60	64	68	62
H_3	64	68	72	76	70
H_4	72	76	80	84	78
Average	60	64	68	72	66

For each genetic variety (row) the successive nutrient mixes (columns) give increasing growth rates, and vice versa. If "good" means fast-growing, then the table has ranked bacterial varieties in the order of *genetic* goodness, and growth media in the order of *nutritional* goodness. It is clear, moreover, what it might mean to say that the effect of "heredity" is twice as great as that of "environment." (The averages listed assign equal weight to all combinations.)

The above example illustrates in a simple way a quite prevalent view of the nature-nurture relationship. I remember being taught it many years ago in a course called "Educational Psychology," as applied to the inheritance of intelligence. There was a "genetic variable" which determined the range of potential intelligence of an individual, and an "environmental variable" which determined the extent to which this potential was realized. The measured intelligence, the phenotype, was then described as a (suitably weighted) linear combination of the two variables. Now of course addition is one of the simplest arithmetical operations, and is very convenient for statisticians. In the bacterial example of Table 1 the rates are given by a simple formula, $R = 8H + 4E + 36$, where H has been assigned the values 1, 2, 3, 4, as has E. In this case we can say that "heredity" is twice as important as "environment." But of course in biological reality there is only one quantitative variable, R, the reproduction rate. The value of this variable depends on the different H's and E's, but these are not representable by numbers, they are much too complex for that. The H's are different combinations or clusters of genetic alleles, of biochemical recipes. The E's are different concentrations of a list of chemical substances, and there is no intrinsic rank-order or measure either of heredity or of environment. The additive quantitative ordering arises from the extremely complex interaction between the growing cell and its environment. The fact that it comes out with simple arithmetical regularity of Table 1 is not very likely, but in this case it can be arranged.

Let me now give another artificial example which, because of the relative simplicity of bacterial genetics, we could arrange with equal ease. Using the same four strains of bacteria, we now compound four new media for them to grow on, with the resulting growth rates shown in Table 2:

TABLE 2

*Purely complementary relationship
between Heredity and Environment.*

	E_1	E_2	E_3	E_4	Average
H_1	54	62	70	78	66
H_2	62	70	78	54	66
H_3	70	78	54	62	66
H_4	78	54	62	70	66
Average	66	66	66	66	66

For each genetic type there is a range of growth rates, depending on nutrition, as before; and for each medium there is equally a range depending on genetic type. But the additive relationship visible in the previous data is now completely gone. Under these circumstances it is impossible to give *any* meaning to the "relative share" or "importance" of heredity and environment in determining growth rates. Here the very question of "relative importance" rests on a false assumption.

To summarize: Table 1 represents an old and still fashionable conception of the relation of nature and nurture, in which any measurable phenotype is described as a sum of "hereditary disposition" and "environmental influence." Heredities, and environments, can be ranked as "good" or "bad" independently of each other. Table 2, equally artificial, represents a situation in which the relative "goodness" or "badness" of heredities, or environments, depends entirely on how they are matched with each other. Here

E_1H_4, E_2H_3, E_3H_2, E_4H_1 are all "best", while E_1H_1, E_2H_4, E_3H_3, and E_4H_2 are "worst." In this case ranking depends on the interaction of heredity and environment. The variables are not additive, as in Table 1, but are *complementary*.

Tables 1 and 2 represent a general format for experimental designs. Whenever it is possible to obtain as many genetically identical individuals of each variety as there are different environments for them to grow in, and to find as many indistinguishable environments as there are genetic varieties, one may investigate the relationships of genetic and environmental variables with respect to any chosen phenotype. Such designs are easiest in plant genetics, and are used in agricultural seed selection, etc. In animal genetics they are harder to realize, both because of the requirement of many genetically identical individuals, and because of the difficulty of saying that two or more environments are the same for different genetic varieties. Animals of different habit may select differently from the same terrain, and this makes the criteria of sameness harder to define.

In most studies of animal, especially human, genetics, one is typically dealing with incomplete information without much experimental control. I shall illustrate below from one kind of study, that of human longevity. A major difficulty is that one lacks information on the proportions of a population to be assigned to various genetic-environmental combinations. One may then be tempted by the simple assumption of a random distribution. But in many cases there is qualitative evidence against such an assumption. Individuals closely related biologically generally tend, for a variety of familiar reasons, to be closely related also in terms of evironmental factors. Thus Galton's studies of "genius" suffer irreparably from the fact that in family and social life especially there is a strong correlation between the genetic and cultural endowments of children. Moreover, what the population geneticists elegantly call "assortive" mating—nonrandom, selective—is in the human case also typically *both* a genetic and a cultural selection.

The central point to be made from my two examples of bacterial growth is that the relationship between genetic and environmental factors can range between, or in various ways combine, the two extremes of additivity and complementarity. I chose the examples from a field where everything is rather well understood, but they are illustrative also of patterns abundantly available from the world of sexual reproduction and, as I shall also point out, from the world of mammalian embryology and specifically of human psychological development. For historical reasons, however, the additivity pattern has long overshadowed the complementarity pattern in the thinking of many persons who have contributed to the statistical theory of populations, to heritability studies, and to the (partial) mathematical elaborations of Darwin's original insights concerning evolution—J. B. S. Haldane, R. A. Fisher, and Sewell Wright. In all these elaborations it is assumed that a certain reproduction rate, or survival value, can be imputed to the genotype, independent of how that genotype manifests itself in the real world of nature-nurture interaction. In other words, additivity has been presupposed.

Evolution itself, on the other hand, requires complementarity; Darwin's central question in *The Origin of Species* concerned the divergence of different species from common ancestry. His explanation of this branching process focused attention on the fact that reproduction rates in *different* environments will favor the survival, in general, of *different* varieties. But this is precisely the situation illustrated in Table 2. Modern evolutionary theory still further emphasizes both the diversity of genetic types within a species, and the diversity of ecological loci within which species may exist. Across a particular range of environments some genetic varieties will reproduce more slowly than others and will tend to be eliminated. But the important kinds of evolutionary change do not happen that way, by the selection of "superiors" over "inferiors."

Indeed any single pure genetic type, however superior in a specific environment, is likely to have a narrow survival *range.* We are learning this in connection with the high-yield grains which have transiently so increased the world's harvest. These have been pure strains and year by year, as a result, such crops have required higher and higher levels of poison to protect them from man's many competitors. In this artificial situation the grasses have been robbed of their genetic diversity and thus of their adaptability, while the predators and parasites have not.

The presence of genetic variety complementary to diverse or fluctuating ecological conditions is absolutely vital to the stability and robustness of a species. As environments change the relative reproduction rates of different varieties may also change—interaction—so that what was dominant becomes rare and what was rare becomes abundant. Only because of this great redundancy of genetic alternatives is it possible to understand how a species can be "preadapted" to some environments which do not yet exist; and that phenomenon is essential to evolutionary theory.

In popular versions of Darwinism the additive assumption, the notion that one can rank genetic types by unqualified "fitness," is always fashionable and is especially characteristic of Social Darwinism. It is expressed directly in the famous catch-phrase of Herbert Spencer, "the survival of the fittest." In a letter to Wallace, Darwin objected to the phrase: "It cannot be used," he said, "as a substantive governing a verb." It is, in other words, a slogan, not a useful concept in the theory of evolution.

Varieties with low general survival value, across all available environments, do indeed occur and are selected against. But their disappearance has little effect on evolution. And except in extremely constant environments no single rare variety, even one with the highest average reproduction rate, has more than a mediocre chance of long-run survival. Chance fluctuations are more likely to eliminate the single "best" in comparison with some out of a great *number* of varieties which are only "pretty good," but otherwise diverse. Variety with complementarity, with many sorts of potential preadaptation, is the steering mechanism of evolution. *Some* of the meek are rather likely to inherit the earth.

In any consideration of the importance of human genetics one must bear in mind the moral of my quasi-realistic examples from bacterial genetics: the "effects of heredity" are in principle undefined except in relation to characteristics of the environment in which an organism develops. In particular, any genetic ordering or quantitative measure of phenotypes is strictly relative to the range of environments across which a given set of genotypes is studied. Across one array of environments bacteria can be ranked in a specific order with respect to growth rates, and that order is invariant to the environmental differences considered. Across another array of environments the picture, for these same genotypes, is completely altered and even the order-invariance of the first case disappears.

Mammalian genetics is of course vastly more complicated, and with special exceptions (such as certain deficiency diseases) we do not know how to modify the immediate biochemical environment of the animal cells. What we call "environmental differences" are of a different order from the controlled nutritional mixes of my examples. There is a much greater genetic and environmental interaction in the long, slow development of complex organisms, arguing against the notion that genetic variety somehow magically produces a strictly parallel phenotypic variety. With respect to traits which are conspicuously plastic (such as those basically affected by learning), the relation is especially complex. One therefore should be sceptical, a priori, about the claim that so manifold a trait as "intelligence" is mainly predetermined by genetic makeup. One wants to look closely at the kinds of evidence and argument offered for such a claim, after defining carefully the kinds of evidence and argument which would validly sustain it. What comes to light then is that the environmental range with respect to which evidence is gathered is absolutely crucial. Rather than go into an extensive discussion*of the technicalities of such matters I have chosen instead to present a parallel case, from the study of human life, where the evidential picture is somewhat more complete, though still affected with major uncertainties. So far as the argument over intelligence is concerned, however, the cases are so essentially parallel that what is obviously true in the one case cannot be rejected in the other without an amount and refinement of evidence which in fact is lacking. The case I have in mind is that of human longevity, about which we possess, from census records around the world and from many special studies, a vast amount of statistical information.

For any sizable human cohort, consisting of a group of persons of the same sex born at about the same period, the mortality picture is as follows. There is at birth a relatively high probability of death per annum, which declines rapidly from birth to a minimum at maturity. From that age the rate again increases slowly but steadily until death has supervened for all members of the cohort. For all large (e.g., national) populations and most subpopulations the adult part of this age-specific mortality curve has one universal characteristic: the probability of death per annum

---

* A concise technical outline of the statistical theory of "heritability" is that of David Layzer, "Heritability Analyses of I.Q. scores: Science or Numerology?" *Science* 183 (29 March 1974), pp. 1259–1266. Layzer's argument against Prof. A. R. Jensen's hereditarian views are tied to theory, evidence, and to questions of methodology. For a recent popular statement of Jensen's own views, see "Race, Intelligence and Genetics: The Differences Are Real," *Psychology Today* 7, (7): 80. For an equally popular counterstatement, see Bruce Wallace, "Genetics and the Great I.Q. Controversy," *The American Biology Teacher* (January 1975).

doubles with a characteristic doubling time of approximately 8.5 years. In some cases where this relation does not quite hold—where the doubling time changes with age—it can be shown that the population in question is a mixture of two identifiable subpopulations each with the characteristic 8.5-year doubling time, of which one has a higher initial death rate (e.g., at age 30) than the other. The second characteristic feature (from special studies) is that age at death appears to be strongly "heritable." Thus identical twins die at much more nearly the same age than siblings (of the same sex), and siblings at much more nearly the same age than unrelated persons, even though the former may lead (after maturity) quite independent lives. If we could study the differences in ages at death of a large number of identical twins separated at birth and scattered randomly over the total range of environments affecting human health, we would have an estimate of the average environmentally determined age at death for pairs of genetically identical individuals. Existing data clearly underestimate, perhaps seriously, that average but give the best estimate we have. Thus for white females beyond the age of 40 the average difference in age at death is about 3.4 years, whereas for unrelated females from the same population it is about 13 years.*

Subject to the caution mentioned, these numbers can be interpreted to imply that about one-quarter of the arithmetic difference in age at death in the female population is

---

* My data are estimates made by Leo Szilard, "On the Nature of the Aging Process," *Proceedings of the National Academy of Sciences*, 45 (Jan. 1959), no. 1, pp. 30–46.

"environmental," while three-quarters is "hereditary." One of the usual interpretations of such a high ratio—about 75 percent for age differences and 90 percent for mean squared differences—is that age at death is genetically fixed; environmental factors have a relatively small influence on the averages. When, however, we look at statistics compiled for various subpopulations, we find large average discrepancies which can be regarded as "mostly hereditary" only on extremely implausible assumptions. Thus a population consisting of college faculties in California at age X has the same death rate as the average of the total white population at age X + 15. In effect the California faculties are 15 years younger in physiological age than the average of their age cohort. In the other direction there is a large black population (about three-quarters of those classified as "nonwhite" in the census) which at age X has the same death rate as the white population at age X − 17. These differences are large by any measure. They are more than the overall adult average age difference at death, and more than one standard deviation, for the population as a whole (above age 40), in opposite directions.* In view of the high degree of heritability cited above it might seem plausible, at first sight, that such group differences must be mainly genetic; for difference in age at death is "mostly hereditary," relatively insensitive to environmental differences which

---

* If one considers life expectancy—the average age to which a cohort at age X survives—these differences are smaller, though conspicuous. The reason is that with advancing age beyond 80 or so, the death *rates* begin to approximate the same value for different groups; for the last 1 percent of the cohort they are almost identical.

prevail within a cohort. Before examining this argument one should, however, take note of a third general fact: There is a universal relationship, over many populations here and abroad, between early environmental insults and deficiencies on the one hand, and adult death rates on the other. In particular, a high infant and childhood mortality rate foreshadows a correspondingly high death rate, at each age, in the adult survivors belonging to that cohort.* A genetic explanation of such facts would require that early health is mainly itself a function of genetic constitution. Such an explanation would finally carry us back to the view that even poverty is mainly a function of genetic constitution—Social Darwinism with a vengeance.

In fact the argument from a high heritability, granting its validity, to a genetic explanation of phenotypic differences between groups is fallacious. Put more charitably, it could be made valid by all the assumptions underlying it if these were made explicit, and were true. One of these is the assumption that we are dealing with a statistically homogeneous population, in particular one in which extreme environmental differences (compared to overall average differences) are rare. In statistical language the distribution of environments, measured in terms of effects on age at death (or any other phenotype) is more or less normal, so that group differences of several standard deviations are

---

* See Hardin B. Jones, "The Relation of Human Health to Age, Place, and Time" in *Handbook of Aging and the Individual*, ed. J. E. Birrens, (Chicago: University of Chicago Press, 1963), p. 41. See also "Demographic Consideration of the Cancer Problem," Transactions of the New York Academy of Sciences, ser. II, vol. 18, no. r, (February 1956), pp. 298–333.

highly improbable and more or less uncorrelated with the defining characteristics of subpopulations within the total population. But this assumption, applied to the U.S. population, is false. Our population is extremely heterogeneous with big average environmental differences between whites, blacks, and various subgroups of these. One consequence of this diversity, in terms of public health and economic status, is that the U.S. ranks well down among the world's nations, along with countries which are on the average much poorer. Yet when we look at the overall U.S. adult vital statistics we see a more or less normal-looking distribution (somewhat skewed) of the numbers dying at each age. The given distribution has the general shape one would predict for a homogeneous population from the assumption of an 8.5-year doubling time of the probability of death per individual. There are some telltale aberrations from the ideal form, but they could be overlooked or misinterpreted. The distribution of environmental differences is indeed not normal and is not uncorrelated with other group differences such as race. So if we take the high heritability ratio discussed above at face value, the evidence points toward the reality of just those extreme differences which an essentially circular argument had wished away.

But that heritability ratio is now further cast in doubt. For it becomes extremely implausible that identical twins or siblings, even if separated early in life, would be likely to sample for us the actual environmental diversity of our society. We are not likely to find one a California college faculty member and the other a farmer in Appalachia, nor one with a white skin and the other black.

I am very far from suggesting that heredity is unimportant in relation to longevity. Recessive lethal genes—genes which are simply inoperative—have a well-established and major effect on mortality, one which is plausibly additive in relation to the effects of nutrition, disease, etc. What I have been criticizing is the misinterpretation of heritability studies which have a very limited range of significance. It is only by illicit arguments that they can be taken to imply, for example, that blacks are essentially shorter-lived than whites. It is fortunate that in the case of longevity we possess enough information to show that these illicit arguments lead to conclusions which are false. To add another example, there is a large (25 percent) black subpopulation in the U.S. (as well as several white ones) which ranks definitely *above* the white average in longevity. There is no reason to conclude that 25 percent of the black population is genetically superior to the whites or to the large black population 75 percent of which ranks so far below it.

A final example of the limited significance of conclusions about "heritability" is the dramatic increase of life expectancy (and decrease in age-specific death rates among adults) in all Western countries over the last seventy-five years. Even a very high heritability is not inconsistent with the obvious fact that these changes are almost entirely due to improved average conditions of nutrition and public health. Populations in a given country (e.g., Sweden) separated by seventy-five years of age are genetically extremely similar but the environmental ranges to which they have been subject in childhood are in recent history radically different. It is simply not possible to argue against a purely environmental interpretation of these differences even on the unproved hypotheses of high heritability.

In discussing the example of longevity I have assumed, perhaps not always correctly, that the H and the E variables involved are in fact additive in their effects. It seems unlikely that there are any genetic constitutions which can thrive on typical kinds of early malnutrition and disease. There is involved moreover, a class of genetic differences —the number of recessive lethal vegetative genes—which will be invariant in their effects to almost all environmental differences. Some cases of complementarity are known, to be sure, such as the genetic deficiencies that promote malarial resistance, and doubtless there are others. Some gross genetic deficiencies are known which can be compensated for by specific medical and dietary provisions. But such phenomena are statistically rare.

Now it happens that the data concerning longevity are quite similar to those concerning I.Q. The average I.Q. for American blacks at the present time is about fifteen points below that for American whites and this is about equal to one standard deviation of I.Q. distribution among whites. The heritability index for I.Q., computed from only slightly less dubious assumptions than in the case of longevity, is about the same; higher in fact for longevity. For the statistically given range of heredities and environments available in the United States, at any rate, it comes out at about 75–80 percent, in comparison with 90 percent for longevity. Assuming as before a homogeneous and normal distribution of environment with respect to their effect on I.Q., one might conclude that if blacks and whites are ge-

62

netically indistinguishable with respect to intelligence, then the actually prevailing black environment must be worse, by several standard deviations, than that affecting whites. But as I have suggested in the parallel case of longevity, it is only the assumption of a homogeneous, normal distribution of environments which gives this argument the appearance of a reduction to statistical absurdity. No one, I think, supposes that black-white differences in age at death among us are primarily genetic. It seems clear that the parallel argument for major genetic I.Q. differences between blacks and whites should fare no better. Both rest in fact on a now-obvious circularity. One first merely *assumes* that environmental conditions sufficient to explain the result are highly improbable, and then concludes that such an explanation is to be rejected.

In the discussion of the statistics of longevity we have been dealing with the kinds of environmental and hereditary differences which are, plausibly, more or less additive in character—with recessive lethal genes and with the effects, in human nuture, of insult and deprivation. Even on similar assumptions regarding I.Q., the existence of major racial-genetic differences with respect to intelligence is so far supported only by invalid argument. I should add, of course, that this same scepticism should be adopted toward the view that any identifiable segment of the white population, which could be large, having the same longevity or I.Q. distribution as American blacks is condemned to that state by its genetic inheritance. A high index of heritability, as statistically defined, simply does not entail that conclusion. But this leads me back to the other type of heredity-environment relationship, that of interaction, or complementarity.

However appropriate the additivity assumption may be to situations we can properly describe in terms of genetic or environmental deprivation, one has the impression that this assumption has seldom been questioned on either side of the nature-nurture debate.* At any rate Professor Arthur Jensen, whose views have done so much to stir up the current cycle of argument, appears to see no other alternative to his own belief in a primarily genetic determination of intelligence, that what he calls "100 percent environmentalist theories."†

In view of all we know about genetics, and especially of new knowledge about the role of the genes of the somatic cells in embryological development, any "100 percent environmentalist" theory of human differences is indeed likely to be wrong unless we mean, as I did in the previous chap-

---

* In the debate started by A. R. Jensen's article "How Much Can We Boost I.Q. and Scholastic Achievement?" appearing in the *Harvard Educational Review*, no. 39, 1969, some critics have concerned themselves with the possibility that interaction phenomena are involved. Notable among these are R. J. Light and P. V. Smith, who in "Social Allocation Models of Intelligence," *Harvard Educational Review*, no. 39, 1969, examine the consequences of assuming that blacks are assigned nonrandomly to environments which react to hinder black intellectual development as compared to that of whites. Their illustrative model was strongly criticized by Professor William Shockley. The continuing debate is to be found in *Review of Educational Research*, 41 (1971), nos. 2, 3, and 4. The Light and Smith model was designed as an internal criticism of Professor Jensen's argument, one which used his own estimates. Professor Shockley's sharp eye finds troubles and implausibilities in it, in a polemical style worthy of the eighteenth century.

† Arthur Jensen, "Heritability and Teachability" in *Individual Differences* (London: Methuen & Co. Ltd., 1973), pp. 398–433; vid. p. 414.

ter, that genetic differences are *minor* in their effects on *cultural* evolution. It is my own view that with respect to important issues of education and social status the genetic differences among us are in fact of special importance. I therefore happily refuse to take a "100 percent environmentalist" position in opposition to Professor Jensen. Where I take issue with Professor Jensen is in his apparent belief that there is a genetically determined quantitative "phenotype" called "intelligence," which is only "modified" by all the processes of embryology and postnatal development. It is this conception which underlies the a priori assumption of additivity. Additivity is justified a posteriori where we have evidence of true genetic weakness, as, for example, in the effect on longevity of recessive lethal alleles. But the predominant case is that of alleles which are simply somewhat different in the enzymes, all equally functional, which they produce. It is within this predominant range that we should make interaction, and the possibility of complementarity, the first order of search. Not a genotype alone, and not an "environment" alone, but a complex system of interactions between them will determine the process and product of development. The phenotype is then *in no way* a kind of "environmentally modified" or distorted image of the genotype, but irreducibly the product of *two* systems of variables and of the tempo and mode of their interaction. In the tradition of thought to which Professor Jensen appears to belong, "interactions"—complementarities—have either been ignored, or have been treated as minor perturbations. As I have indicated already, the very basis of Darwinian evolution is destroyed by this outlook, which implies not only that there is genetic selection within given environments, but also a selection of environments by genetic varieties viable in them.

It is thus necessary to see clearly that genetic *difference* is not genetic *inequality*. Inequality is not in any sense a genetic attribute, but only applies to rankable or measurable phenotypes. What is true of genetic difference is that when genetic varieties are subject, hypothetically, to the same environment, phenotypes in general develop unequally. What is also true, however, is that in suitably different shared environments, the measures and even the rank-ordering of phenotypes will be altered. If we don't produce such a result, we simply haven't tried very hard. The variety of environments which will produce such radical changes may be more or less available, and may or may not show up in natural demographic samples, especially when the ability to discriminate significant environmental differences sharply is lacking. It is possible, indeed, that the environmental conditions which would maximize average longevity, or I.Q., or musicianship, in two groups such as blacks and whites, would be somewhat different. Thus blacks might have higher I.Q.'s than whites in one sort of environment which both shared, and the reverse in another. Such complementarity is known to hold in some cases affecting longevity. The sickle-cell syndrome, mentioned above, is far more prevalent among blacks than whites. It protects against certain malarias, though it is fatal in homozygous form. In malarial environments it is presumably selected for, in nonmalarial environments, against.

But the basic importance of complementarity lies in the

observation that for each individual there is, in principle, a pathway of development which will optimize certain valuable characteristics, one in principle different from that which will optimize those same traits in another individual. It is thus possible to think, for example, that genetically different individuals may develop, in appropriately different environments, in ways which would bring them all to the condition of being equally valuable though different musicians, or mathematicians, or political leaders. The demonstration of such a possibility would force us to abandon the traditional but genetically implausible view that there are "born" musicians, mathematicians, statesmen, and thus in an unexpected way to find a new basis for the concept of equality.

In the next chapter it is my intent to follow up the implications of two themes introduced in this one. The first theme is the recognition that additivity in nature-nurture relationships is a special case, and that in the general case the working assumption of additivity should be replaced by that of a nonadditive, interactive relationship, except where heredities, or environments, can properly be described in globally positive or negative terms. In extending the theme of interaction and complementarity I shall try to look more closely at some postnatal developmental phenomena which have only been hinted at in the present chapter.

The second theme which has been introduced here, in connection with the criticism of views of the genotype-phenotype relationship which have prevailed until recently, is the need to question systematically the kind of statistical assumption that underlies the orthodox logic of heritability arguments, when that logic is applied to intelligence and other comparably plastic human traits. In questioning the way in which Jensen reduces the "100 percent environmentalist" view of intelligence to improbability or absurdity, I was simply expressing scepticism, pointing out that he appeals to a wholly untested and implausible assumption of statistical homogeneity and normality in the distribution of relevant environmental influences. In the sequel I intend to set forth positive arguments as to why this assumption should be doubted, and what sort of alternative assumption should be put in its place; one proper, namely, to cumulative processes.

In the development of these themes my main purpose will be to suggest some of the implications of these two themes for the theory and practice of education, and to lay some groundwork for a viable egalitarian ethic.

CHAPTER FOUR

ABILITIES AND TALENTS

———

WHEN IT COMES to the uniquely human characteristics we call abilities and talents there is especially good reason to doubt that these can be thought of, in their individual variety among us, as simply reflections of a corresponding genetic variety. This necessary doubt is not to question the degree to which this sort of genetic determinism holds; what needs to be questioned is the conception itself. The analysis so far does not suggest, however, that our genetic variety is negligible in importance. What it suggests is that now-traditional genetic thinking is simplistic and often wrong in the way it conceives the nature-nurture relationships involved.

Nor should it be supposed that I am questioning the genetic determinism which underlies our essential biological characteristics as distinct from other species. We are *born* as members of a species uniquely apt for culture and for cultural evolution, and there is nothing "environmental" about that. In that sense, as I pointed out in reviewing classical modern ideas on equality (chapter two), we are at that level all essentially equivalent to each other and essentially different from other species, at least other existing species. But in that sense also we are uniquely, in all our human attainments, the expression of a nonbiological history, the evolution of culture.

In saying this one must, of course, set aside all those gross genetic defects which prevent development or inhibit it across all developmental environments—doubly missing genes or chromosomal abnormality, for example. No doubt there is, in our existing state of knowledge, a considerable gray area between what may be called normal genetic variety and what should be called gross deficiency, or syndrome. Some deficits may of course be compensated for by chemotherapy or by educational therapy. Still I think we should not for theoretical purposes disregard such an obvious distinction—keeping it open to emendation in the light of new knowledge. The normal range is, in my view, the general range of genetic variety in which some kind of nature-nurture complementarity is known or can be found to prevail.

Let me illustrate. In an earlier John Dewey Lecture Professor Theodosius Dobzhansky expressed much the sort of scepticism expressed here about racial and other large-group differences in intelligence, and surely based on great scientific experience in the field.* It troubles me, however, that Professor Dobzhansky is willing to discuss such a thing

* *Genetic Diversity and Human Equality* (New York: Basic Books, 1973).

as musical talent as though it were clearly a genetic, that is, polygenic, trait. He is perfectly aware of the existence of nature-nurture "interactions," complementary relationships in development. Yet he discusses the way in which musicians, being attracted to each other, could by intermarriage greatly increase the local concentration of some genetic complexion which was especially apt for musicianship. But the concept of music is not a biological one at all, and there can be no genes or combinations of genes which are literally "for" music. Music is a product of culture, though its roots are I am sure very old. As human beings we are all apt for music in a way different from other species, songbirds included. But that is to say that, in the sense of chapter two, musicianship characterizes us all, in principle, and is thus independent of our genetic variety. When it comes to the locally important differences among us in this respect, however, we are talking about skills and commitments at a very high level of learning and organization, a level where there *are* obviously other sources than the genetic for the information of our capacities. There may of course be relevant genetic defects. Tone deafness may be a candidate, though I know of no research which says it cannot be remedied. Absolute pitch (perhaps impossible for many genetic constitutions) is at least as useful for musicality as a tuning fork or an Accutron watch.

What I do not in the least doubt is that in a given milieu, and subject to *similar* musical inducements and instructions, we will in fact display talents, and develop them, in very unequal degree. But so likewise, I urge, different kinds of children—different genetically and in human nurture

73

and early choice—become musical along *different* pathways and yet grow to be equal in merit as musicians. As in the case of my hypothetical bacteria in chapter two, H_1 and H_4 can have the same musical "growth rate" but perhaps they will do so only if matched, respectively, to some complementary E_4 and E_1. Obviously I do not *know* that there is this kind of complementarity in the genesis of musical talent, or that it exists over a wide range of genetic variety. But I wish in this chapter to make that sort of possibility appear both reasonable and important. Thesis: We can learn equally in any area of human concern and value but only, in general, if there is some provision that we can learn differently.

The view that I wish to develop is thus neither the common view of the inheritance of talent, nor the "100 percent environmentalist" view that our genetic variety has nothing to do with the case. To be sure the fact that an elaborate domain, such as the peculiarly human world of music, is culturally evolved does imply that it is deeply and widely rooted in the human population and in that respect independent of internal genetic variety. In the matter of conspicuous individual talents, however, the view I am suggesting is that these can be the product of most genetic varieties of persons, if nurtured in a musical environment responsive to the temperament, style and evolving life course which each may happen, constitutionally, to represent.

In the perspective of scientific investigation of such matters, statistical studies of natural populations have a limited usefulness. For H_1 the environmental factors E_4 favorable to the development of talent may be abundant and easily defined; for H_4 the corresponding E_1 may be relatively uncommon, or it may not be obvious and so unidentified, its effects diluted or masked by statistical "noise."

In particular, we need a framework of general ideas adequate to the developmental perspective in which all important abilities and talents should be viewed. This means that we should dig under the surface of those tests which have provided the empirical basis for so much of statistical psychometrics, and specifically the various intelligence tests which are presupposed in the debate to which the previous chapter was addressed. I do not want to beat the I.Q. tests over the head. They are useful in their way, though as John Dewey said more than once, they are of little use to good teachers, who need both a refinement and an immediacy of discrimination in their daily work with children which global test averages do not provide.

Having said that I will not beat the I.Q. over the head, I cannot resist a little story, about two Indian children in New Mexico, which came my way while writing this. My friend's job required that she administer such a test, the WISC Weschler Information Subtest for children. Question: What are the four seasons in the year? Wrong answer: Elk hunting, deer hunting, bear hunting, and fishing. Second child, another question: Who discovered America? Wrong answer: *We* did. The human mind is indeed remarkable. But I do not wish to enter the debate over the "cultural fairness" of tests. The bigger question is not that of the choice of test items; it is the question of intelligence-fairness, the fairness of such measures to the concept of intelligence required by an adequate theory.

Which way should we look for a deeper theory of ability or intelligence? There are many ways of approaching this question. In my second chapter I have already chosen to start from the very large historical fact of man's unique biological ability to modify his own existence, to be the inventor, transmitter, and receiver of the fruits of cultural evolution; indeed to *be* that fruition. That is the first approximation. Within that range of basic equality we are genetically diverse and diverse also by environment and experience. We are able to weave together the many strands of biological and cultural inheritance, each time in novel ways. The process and product of this weaving express a general aptitude of which all talents are species, an aptitude for the development of individuality. We shape our own knowledge and conduct, and we celebrate the shaping. In doing so we must indeed assimilate what others before us have learned and invented, but we do so in our own style and to our own ends. The aptitude is native and universal, but the content, the evolving person or agent, is not. From the moment of birth each individual is committing himself in some directions, withdrawing in others; elaborating some skills and talents, leaving others undeveloped; coming to common human concerns and knowledge along different pathways, then branching out again in different ways.

In such a perspective our double inheritance, biological and cultural, serves a vital material role, but one not in any strict sense determinative. Children who are constantly hungry or fearful do not learn well, nor do children who subsist in narrow environments, natural and human. Some causal conditions are thus necessary for a good life, but they do not explain it. We do not explain, adequately describe, human biographies in such wholly causal terms. Explanations of that kind are always interestingly incomplete or lamely retrospective, whether offered by Freudians or by Skinnerians. One can always push them further, but the attempt to explain invention or achievement is increasingly ad hoc as one pursues it, less science than doctrinal habit.

And yet just here is where theory is needed, needed to define the functional significance of such concepts as talent, ability, intelligence.

Let me draw a parallel. We have in modern molecular genetics a well-organized basic account of the means of transmission, from generation to generation, of that vast amount of biological instruction by which each generation gives form and vitality to those new growing assemblages of chemical matter which thereby become its offspring. In animal organisms this process of genetic instruction becomes increasingly complex in the nature-nurture interactions that mediate it, and much of that embryology is still only slightly understood. In cultural evolution we have, I suppose, a similar distinction to draw. If we think of education, in the broadest sense, in terms of the metaphor or concept of *transmission*, looking only from one mature generation to the next, we are looking at the process from a point of view analogous to that of the classical geneticist, who takes the phenotypic character as the expression of what has been transmitted from a previous generation. When however we look at the *process* of intellectual development we see that "transmission" must be replaced by a more complex conception of the interaction between the apparatus of thought and action which infants and children bring to the educative situation, and that which is brought to it by adults who, purposefully or otherwise, play the part of teachers. *What* children assimilate and add to their repertoires of thought and action is not related in any simple or automatic way to the intent of the teacher. From this point of view human culture is not so much transmitted as, in each generation, reconstructed. Just as variety in the biological phenotype is not in general simply the expression of genotypic variety, so the knowledge and habitude of one generation is not simply the expression of what the previous generation "transmitted" to it.

Thus in their education human beings are not passive, directed in their learning by external social processes. Nor is their learning something which mysteriously unfolds from within, stimulated but undirected from without. In *Democracy and Education,* and *Experience and Education,* Dewey gives a nice analysis of the way in which each of these views derives sustenance from the errors of the other, while both are committed to the fallacy of "either-or."

In education there is really nothing corresponding to the genetic code (not even the textbook!). As many have observed, cultural evolution is Lamarckian, the transmission of characteristics which are acquired through human inventiveness, and in being passed on are always open to further modification. Education is at once the genetics and the embryology of culture. And in the theory of education we are deficient. I mean theory in the scientific sense, of well-unified knowledge which commands a professional consensus.

But if we are to develop that sort of theory we must unpack what it means to say that educationally significant learning and development are not "passive." We must speak concretely of the human capacity for self-direction and choice in learning, in learning about the world and about ourselves, the learning which goes to shape and organize our conduct and our further learning. We must speak about this generic human capacity not because it is something we are morally or politically in favor of, but because without self-direction and choice not much learning ever takes place. And in speaking about these generic capacities we must look at them developmentally and in their cumulative effects, in terms of what Dewey called the Continuum of Experience. Everything learned along the course of this continuum is stored in some way and its effect is always to modify the course of further experience. The essential tool of learning is the knowledge we can retrieve for new use, and it is only so that we can order our experience or extend it. When we talk about human abilities, therefore, we are of necessity talking about something which incorporates the product of antecedent learning, not the learning of isolated facts but learning understood as the central process in the continuum of experience, as the builder of the mind's reference library, and the architect of its character structure.

It is in this context that we must understand also the mind's extraordinary capacity to assimilate, to appropriate, and to reorganize so much of what others in the past have learned, to be the receiver of transmitted knowledge, and error. It was Dewey again who cut through the apparent contradiction of the mind's active and autonomous role in learning through interaction with the primary environment, and its apparently passive role as receiver of preorganized and precodified knowledge and tradition. The resolution requires that we recognize the inseparability between equality and fraternity, between individuality and community. We learn in contexts of associated endeavor in which the knowledge possessed by some is expressed, is externalized in relation to problematic situations jointly shared. This expression or externalization is far more than verbal communication; nor is it "training."

When we think about the general concept or category of intelligence from this point of view, it represents particularly what we need to know about each other in order to organize our shared endeavors for educational efficiency and success. One must select the level of one's association and communication, and its material milieu, in such a way that what one expresses or enacts, in that milieu, is in fact accessible for use and assimilation by another. In the particular mode of association which we have formalized as education—but remembering Dewey's penetrating suggestion that every institution can be judged by its educative value—this requires of a teacher that he or she select or design an environment, for shared endeavor, which is matched to the learning capacities, complementary to the talent or manifest intelligence, if you wish, of the learner. The judgment of intelligence which a teacher needs is first of all a qualitative judgment, it is a judgment of kind before it can usefully be a judgment of degree. It is only through such qualitative judgment that a teacher can begin to come to terms with children's individuality, and thus reach toward and plan for that which will invite and steady them to make some significant investment in learning. Such judgments, as made by skillful and successful teachers, are probably the best and most refined evidence we have, at the present time, concerning the developmental morphology of human individuality and human intelligence.

The priority of qualitative discrimination over quantitative measure means that what a teacher is concerned with is in the nature of a profile defined over many different kinds of potential skill or talent, a profile with many dimensions. Let me draw such a profile in polar coordinates, in which each direction represents some distinctive talent or ability.

You will notice that the graph I have drawn is very uneven (see figure 1); it suggests high competence in some directions and rudimentary ability in others. Such contrasts do not define individuality, but they are characteristic of it. We are almost all rather able in some respects, remarkably so in a few, and at the same time remarkably lacking in others.

Remember please that I am talking about concretely defined abilities of the sort a teacher or colleague would notice, not some abstract theoretical scheme such as psychologists have constructed by statistical factor analysis. The wide range implied in my first graph is intended to reflect a general characteristic of what we ordinarily call abilities or talents, to reflect something we know generally about de-

Figure 1
*An Imaginary Profile of Concrete Abilities;
A Two-Dimensional Projection.*

velopmental phenomena. The statistical distribution of such phenomena with respect to magnitude does not fit the familiar normal, bell-shaped curve dear to the elementary textbooks on statistics. We find the latter curve in nature whenever a magnitude attained is (or is approximated by) the algebraic sum of many independent random impulses. But there is another law of distribution, one frequently found in the domain of biology; each additional impulse of growth has an effect which is proportional to the growth already achieved. It is the statistical law of snowballs, which grow more rapidly as they get bigger. It is the law reflected in the maxim that to him that hath it shall be given, and is mundanely reflected in most social distributions of income, severely skewed in the direction of large incomes, with the mode well below the arithmetic mean, and a supernormal variance (see figure 2).

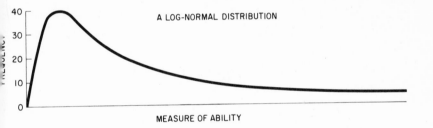

Figure 2
The Log-Normal Distribution

Such distributions have a standard ideal mathematical form defined by the assumption that each impulse of growth multiplies what is already there by a random amount slightly greater, on the average, than one. The result is the logarithmically normal function. The distribution is stock-in-trade for growth phenomena: bacterial colonies, trees, and, I claim, the talents of children.

If what I have called abilities or talents grow in this way, then any theoretically adequate measure of the mind's growth in a specific direction should have this radically skewed, log-normal distribution. Think of artists and their kin, of academic occupations, analytic and discursive; think of the various forms of social praxis, in private life and public. Think of the wisdom of the streets, in which slum children must excel; of the strategic skills of creative mathematicians, or those of Felix Krull the confidence man. Each such specific skill or talent is a system of what the Greeks would have called virtues; it has an organic character, a higher-order organization of lower-order elements of tuned perception, tuned behavior, and of readiness to act, analyze, and learn.

In suggesting a theoretical case for the log-normal distribution of specific human talents I could surely do worse than quote from the excellent analysis of Professor Jensen, in an essay on the study of individual differences. In this essay Professor Jensen is concerned with underlining the importance of the study of individual difference as basic to the investigation of human learning, as opposed to the view more common among psychologists, that such differences are just a nuisance. In any highly composite structure of more elementary components the natural variety of those components and of the ways they go together may give us important clues for the testing of hypotheses about the elements and their composition. As a philosopher of science I am in hearty agreement. An obvious example is provided in the early modern history of chemistry, where it was the variety of chemical structures, even of the same elements, which finally provided evidence about the nature of those structures and the literal elements that compose them. In

84

Jensen's language, it was the study of "I.D.'s" which provided the decisive evidence.

In Jensen's view the original elements are primitive psychophysical learning abilities which he would seek to define. He thinks of these, as they may vary from individual to individual, as "genotypes," presumably independent factors underlying mental ability which the psychology laboratory might hope to isolate and study, or to infer from the intercorrelations among scores on laboratory tests. In his view what are usually called mental abilities are already at a level of organization above these inherited native learning abilities, and that organization itself is learned. Even abilities which psychologists have considered primary may prove to belong to this secondary or derivative level. And here I quote:

An inevitable and complicating fact we must contend with is that learning abilities also grow out of learning itself. This fact is perhaps best conceptualized in terms of a complex hierarchy of transfer functions. In theory basic learning abilities, on the one hand, and abilities attributable to transfer from earlier learning, on the other, must constitute a true dichotomy, since something has to be learned initially and some primitive, basic abilities must be present to accomplish this. Beyond a very early stage of life, however, we are forced to think of these basic learning abilities as an idealized point at one end of a continuum of types of learning in which transfer, learning sets, mediational systems, and the like play an increasingly important role as we move along the continuum. For practical purposes, such as the understanding of ID's in school learning, in problem solving, and in the acquisition of complex skills, the study of transfer hierarchies will be of paramount importance. Basic learning abilities will, of course, be manifested in the sense that they will underlie the rate of acquisition of learning sets, mediational systems, and the like. At the same time, the development of these systems will also facilitate the acquisition of other systems in the hierarchy. The more elemental learning processes and abilities may become thoroughly camouflaged under the elaborate overlay of transfer functions.*

I quote this statement at length because it puts so strongly the complexity of interrelation between what is native and what is learned, and the impossibility of conceiving late-stage talents and abilities as mere expressions of what is there to begin with—not at all a "genotype," but itself a product of equally complex embryological development. Indeed since the embryology of the nervous system is still incomplete at birth we must also take very seriously the interaction of learning and late-stage embryology.†

Professor Jensen here suggests, consistent with his more familiar views, that the elementary "genotypes" of native learning ability must somehow determine the rate of the whole hierarchical development, and thus by implication such rate-measures as the I.Q. But unless he denies further statistical variability in the learning process itself, as that depends on environmental factors, it seems to me he has left very little room for asserting the view for which he has become well known, that intelligence is mostly hereditary in an additive sort of way. Indeed this concession is suggested, unless I misinterpet it, in the final sentence quoted.

In any case this description of the interaction of native

* Arthur R. Jensen, *Educational Differences* (London: Methuen & Co. Ltd, 1973), pp. 339–340.
† See Holger Hydèn, "Biochemical Approaches to Learning and Memory" in *Beyond Reductionism*, ed. Arthur Koestler and J. R. Smythies (Boston: Beacon Press, 1969).

learning ability with learning itself, given the fact of statistical variability all along the developmental path, seems to me a very clear demand for something like the snowball law of distribution, in any population, with respect to specific high-order human abilities. Given the fact of variability in primitive or native learning abilities, Professor Jensen's statement further suggests the possibility of *divergent* pathways of development and, unless matched by complementary environmental influences, unequal attainments along different dimensions of talent—the rosette profile.

Let me reemphasize that this profile of abilities or talents represents the achieved competence of a human being at a particular time, and is not to be confused with representations of intelligence as a function of numerous more special abilities on which it may depend such as memory span, verbal abilities, etc. This rosette profile in fact represents, but for my purposes far more adequately, the same *sort* of information about individuals as is conveyed by intelligence tests, and the question naturally arises as to why the statistical distribution of I.Q. scores shows none of the radical skewness characteristic of growth statistics. Let me suggest what I think is the answer. If you were deliberately to sample numerous small items of competence from across the whole uneven rosette profile, or even any reasonable sector of it, putting these together as separate items on a psychometric test, you would in fact obtain a distribution much less skewed and rather close to the familiar bell-shaped distribution. Some snippets of knowledge or skill would be common to abilities developed along different rays in the profile, but they would not be statistically dependent on each other in such a way as to give rise to the log-normal, snowball law of distribution. If one looks at psychometric tests such as existing intelligence tests from this point of view, the normal distribution they provide is nothing of deep significance; it is merely an artifact of the prevailing principles of test design.

Let me suggest a comparison familiar to college teachers. It is the difference between a technically well-designed multiple choice examination of the sort which still bears the honorific name of "objective," to be inexpensively graded for large classes, and a technically well-designed essay examination, in which a thoughtful discussion of matters defined in question one lays the basis for coming to grips with what is asked for in question two, and so on. When a student who has learned well has finished this sort of test, he or she is surprised to realize that the examination has a kind of cumulative character and has fitted things together in a synopsis in which new global connections have been discerned. Such an examination is itself educative. Questions on the "objective" examination, on the other hand, must be numerous, brief, unambiguous, unarguable, and sterile. But it can be given a score untouched by human minds, and this score will have statistical reliability, which means that if two hundred questions were randomly divided into two one-hundred-question examinations, the two scores for a given student would probably not differ by more than a few points. The student cannot argue about his grade and it probably doesn't occur to him to argue about the design of the examination, after all it is "fair." The sequential essay examination, by contrast, has to be read by someone who is a well-informed teacher and critic, and who always has difficulty with assigning grades or even in ranking papers, especially mediocre ones. The proper response would not be a grade, but a far greater amount of information, a critical paragraph. The grade if required is not "objective," though it can be defensible. Judged not by numbers but by the teacher's personal response, it has a wide range, from high appreciation to self-critical despair. It just doesn't feel like a "normal distribution." Its parts are not logically independent, and a student who can't cope with question one will have a hard time getting beyond it.

But I don't immediately propose any quantitative psychometric test on the growth-model design. If what I propose is testable by "hard data"—inexpensive data—that must come in some other form. But the rosette, log-normal growth model does have other implications. It corresponds, in the first place, to the kind of diagnostic pictures which a teacher should attempt to construct in planning for the inevitable diversity of any specific group of children. To be effective a teacher needs to look for and define the areas and kinds of strength which each child may already possess, and at the same time to define directions in which each is immature or seemingly unready to learn. These readings of a child's present character and direction are a necessary source of suggestion for how just *this* child can be directed toward new subject matter, how the strengths can be made available to overcome the weaknesses. Above all, a teacher must be working at that sort of portraiture in every effort to help children extend and deepen their range of self-direction and choice in learning. Every success a teacher enjoys in such planning brings partial confirmation of the portrait's likeness to the child, and every failure brings new evidence to modify the portrait. Looked at from this point of view the I.Q. is indeed not of much use to a teacher. The raw subscores on I.Q. subtests would be more useful, and their usefulness would be greatly enhanced by careful observation and analysis of a child's conduct through the testing situation. What would be learned in this way could be a useful check on the much richer portrait which a teacher could have built over many days' association in a rich and busy classroom.*

Those judgments of intelligence, knowledge, and character which we need to make in all serious associations, and especially in successful teaching, are inherently, I think, of the kind my graphs are intended to suggest. A child's specific kinds of strength—things which have already engrossed him and have brought knowledge, skill, imagination with them—are the foundations on which he can, with direction and support, design what may be called transfer capacities, ways in which knowledge and confidence in one sort of activity may inform and encourage the child's learning in other important areas.

There is a characteristic feature of developmental and evolutionary processes, an "almost" law, which is the pervasive fact of unevenness. Some children teach themselves to walk at nine months, some only at twice that age. Like the I.Q., the W.Q. (Walking Quotient) varies widely.

* I owe this observation to Frances Hawkins, a teacher of young children with many years' experience.

Some begin the systematic practice of language with single words, then two or more in grammatical combinations, far earlier than others. High L.Q.! Some, where books are valued, will similarly begin to teach themselves to read in the second or third year, while others will be occupied elsewhere until a much later age. One may look for "causes" of such differences and sometimes plausibly find them in the richness or poverty of an environment, in the way parental values and provisions are manifest, in specific developmental (and sometimes identifiably genetic) characteristics. Where one or a few such traits are overvalued that is likely to produce a generalizing judgment, that one child is fast or bright, another slow or dull. Such judgments are endemic in much of our early schooling, where a constrained environment and a narrowly prescribed curriculum almost guarantee overvaluing. I.Q. tests and the like, imported from the psychology laboratory, are statistically correlated with such judgments, and tend to reinforce them. But the I.Q. did not create such tunnel vision, which was there already. What it very often does, however, is to drape such judgments, the projection of a school's failure, in the flag of science. The correlation of I.Q. tests with prevailing measures of school achievement is itself a result, I have suggested, of the fact that I.Q.-ish test items are sampled from a limited sector of the complete profile of a child's style, talent, and knowledge. If two children are of low achievement within that sector but are very different in levels or patterns of ability outside of it, they will not in general be distinguished but will be equally doomed to failure along the single track which school mainly provides.

It is in following this line of analysis that we come back, at a new level, to the importance of complementarity. This time the complementarity is something to be sought, a design of teaching through the mediation of experience which matches a child's "readiness." The old and familiar concept of readiness in itself usually restricted to one prejudiced dimension, however, as in rubrics like "reading readiness." A child who is not already well on the way toward teaching himself to read is typically not "ready" for standard school reading instruction, which too often focuses on the use of methods which restrict this humane art to the dimensions of a mechanical decoding skill. On the other hand, a child not "ready" by this criterion may be fully ready, along unique roads and pathways he has already used and mapped well, to encounter and begin to decipher the storybook or the reference book—books that will have positive valence in the context of that child's life. The question should not be the blanket one of whether a child is "ready" to read, but of how, or along what tracks of growth, and at what pace, *can* the art and the addiction to it best be learned. The question is not *whether* a child is ready for some standard reading method, but rather, at any time, what the child *is* ready for. With such diagnostic questions in mind a teacher can, by successive approximation, design a pathway toward reading which (among other aims) tends to optimize, for each, his involvement with the world of books.

More generally, designs for teaching which take fullest possible advantage of the jagged profile of each person's talents and abilities will be richer and more diversified than standard academic tracks, providing both for wide qualitative differences in individuals and also for significant and self-revealing choice by individuals. This view is sharply at odds with many tendencies in present-day efforts to improve schooling, including prepackaged curricula which, in the guise of helping teachers, rob them of initiative and responsibility for working to achieve diversity and flexibility. It is especially at odds with that tendency to ignore context which is evident in absolutist labels such as "dyslexia," "hyperactivity," and the rest. With rare exceptions these terms are used in the manner of Molière's famous joke about the "dormitive virtue" which explains the effect of morphine, an explanation in the present case which only baptizes something wrong in the *relations* of the school to a particular child by imputing it as a *property* of the child alone, a syndrome. I should observe that there is nothing in the rosette profile, or the need for ways of teaching responsive to its indications, which excludes the possibility for recognizing what is genuinely to be classed as syndrome; something calling for clinical reference and treatment, limitations on a child's learning which a school simply cannot, even with the greatest art, transform to positive advantage. It is often only when such efforts have been seriously made, on the contrary, that genuine physical or psychogenic barriers can be defined. It is also true, moreover, that the anticipation of failure stemming from visible or medically well-defined symptoms may itself be a cause of that failure. Even some of the gross genetic defects (such as chromosomal abnormality) which commonly seem to limit learning can be put in this doubtful list.

In the context of today's agonizing debate over the failure of many children to learn even the rudiments (the traditional three R's), and over the tendency of many more to develop the spiritless habit of "getting by," it is time to search deeply for every limitation which may match and unwittingly sanction the practical limitations and resulting demoralization of the educational system we have evolved. I have been concerned to undercut one of these, the assumption that human talents and abilities are somehow genetically determined, at least up to an additive and relatively minor variability associated with social nurture and educative influence. I have suggested a quite different system of ideas which recognizes the standard assumption above only as a limiting case.

Those responsible for early education will always, in the way of thinking I urge, seek to provide for children a human and natural environment complementary to their constitutions and their development to date. Failure will not be imputed to children as a property, but as a relation. It will be analyzed as evidence to guide new efforts toward success.

The argument of this chapter leads, if one follows it, to a certain refinement of the omnibus term "environment." For bacteria environment means simply a chemical or biological soup at a given temperature. For higher animals it means much more. At any level one must include, under the term, both the selectivity of the organism and the reaction of the environment to the organism's behavior. Genetically different cattle, in the same pasture, will select somewhat different fodder. Are these then different environments? At one level they are, at another they are not. The environment of a predator involves the defense reactions and strategies of his prey, that of a grazing animal in the same territory involves the strategies of the predator. At the level of human learning one child elicits one set of reactions from parent or teacher, another elicits a very different set.

Thus an infant who from birth is placid and "good" may often be left unstimulated, and patterns of human interchange may remain rudimentary. Another child of the same parents may be lively and demanding, and elicit responses which, chain-like, lead to a far richer channel of communication. In another family these patterns may be reversed, the lively one being put off or antagonized, the placid one given great attention, so that again the matrix of communication develops well.*

Is it then impossible to define a *generally* good environment? The answer is no on one level, yes on another. Clearly such an environment must be described as possessing not only a diversity or richness of opportunities for different children's involvement in natural and human affairs, but has also the kind of responsiveness to their early probings and strivings which is able to diagnose and plan for their general and individual learning. Here the interaction is at its most complex, where the environment includes adults who are the intelligent coagents of children's learning.

---

* Sibylle Escalona, *The Roots of Individuality*, (Chicago: Aldine Publishing Co, 1968). This is one of the not numerous reports of research and analysis which digs deeply beneath the surface of the conventional classifications of early childhood influence on development, and the example above is a kind of interaction—complementarity—she discusses.

In the discussion of the concept of complementarity, and of planned interaction, I should mention that this emphasis has recently been much examined and somewhat investigated by educational researchers. The general research scheme is to group children in terms of various test criteria, and then to seek an appropriately complementary teaching strategy for each group. If "aptitude-treatment interaction" is realizable, then group A should do better than group B with one "treatment," group B better than group A by the other. To emphasize again my lack of total disagreement with Professor Arthur Jensen, I should mention that he has taken this idea seriously.*

I should also mention that strong general arguments for making such investigations were first advanced by Professor Lee Cronbach,† and the trade has responded well. So I do not feel quite alone. The results of such investigations as have been made so far are generally unimpressive; there are no shouts of "Eureka! I found it!" I think the appropriate response, in an-Archimedean Greek, rather, is "Apolusa— I lost it." But in such matters failure to demonstrate is not of much evidential value. The typical "interaction" investigation, to date, is only a tiny step along the way I urge here.‡ The concept of interaction in teaching is as old as

* See especially Arthur Jensen, Op. Cit., Chapter 1.

† L. J. Cronbach, "How Can Instruction Be Adapted to Individual Differences?" in R. M. Gagné (ed.), *Learning and Individual Differences* (Columbus, Ohio: Charles E. Merrill, 1967.) A later book by Cronbach, (it is now in press and I have not yet seen it) is J. L. Cronbach and R. E. Snow, *Aptitude and Instructional Methods* (New York: Irvington Press, in press).

‡ Two reviews of such research are D. C. Berliner and L. Cahen, "Trait Treatment Interaction and Learning," *Review of Research in Education,*

the hills among experienced practitioners, and is implicit in all notions of readiness, talent, individuality. Still it is good that educational research is catching up. I believe that the power of "interactive" teaching *can* be demonstrated within the halls of academe, as it has many times in the experience of highly successful teachers—but the demonstration will require a refinement of discrimination among "types" of children which is virtually the equivalent of that exercised by the most skillful teachers, and which is likely to define as many "types" as there are children involved—requiring also an equivalent diversity of "treatments". Surely a four-fold sorting of many children, grouped in two types and accorded two treatments, will be unlikely to do it. As physicists would say, there is too much "noise" in such experimental designs to yield impressive evidence. One should sympathize. It is not easy to demonstrate some of the key things that good practitioners know. To suppose otherwise would be arrogant. It may even require a better paradigm of research than the one now dominant. Before we get to the stage of statistical proofs of basic truths in education, we might be better advised to go to the practitioner, as Darwin did to the animal breeders. One is tempted to urge, "Go to the teacher, thou scientist!"

The prevailing methodology of educational research is derived from the nineteenth-twentieth century expansion of a body of statistical theory which has found its greatest pay-off in fields like agricultural research. In such fields one can

1973, 1, 58–94, and "Achievement Treatment Interactions," *Review of Educational Research*, 46, 1 (Winter 1976) 61–75.

succeed in measuring or classifying many individuals in terms of a relatively small number of a priori significant dimensions. For educational research this approach begs the basic question: how to *find* and *define* what the basic dimensions in fact are. It is the definitions of these dimensions which requires that we go to the successful practitioners, not casually or occasionally but with a long-term commitment. Is such research allowed, today, for the best graduate students? Not often. What then is the new paradigm? If it must be formalized, the formalities lie in a little-developed part of statistical theory. Here the problem is not how to classify many individuals according to a few dimensions, but to classify a few individuals according to many dimensions. The common-sense way of doing this is the insightful case-history, the personal distillation of experience. One can also call it ethology or ethnography, and often the "subjects" of such research are co-authors. But there is a latent statistical theory about this, concealed by the stereotype belief that it is only a primitive or first-stage sort of process. The beginnings of theory which I refer to lie in the domain of pattern recognition and information theory, and its product is a distillation of new concepts, often hard-won, which will *then* support significant and useful theory. Its problem is not yet the analysis of data, but the knowledge of how to get data that are worth analyzing.

In the last chapter I shall be returning to the central topic of equality: trying for a more adequate definition, based upon the idea of coagency developed here, and generalized as a basic explication of the third term in the classical trinity—liberty, equality, fraternity.

CHAPTER FIVE

THE ETHICS OF

EDUCATION

———

IN THIS CHAPTER I wish to suggest a definition of human equality as something neither guaranteed nor excluded by our general biological equality or our specific biological diversity, but possible of attainment, by successive approximation, in a society which commits itself to that goal. Such a commitment is implicit in our ethical traditions, but we have qualified it in practice by quite other and often incompatible directions of social development and by counterclaims that equality is really impossible to achieve. If the crudities of Social Darwinism are more or less discredited, they still crop up again in subtler versions.

The definition of equality I propose is more complex than that of the political classics, or that of my first conclusion (in agreement with the classics), namely, that our de facto inequalities of status and ability are essentially non-biological but originate in the uneven dynamics of social development, including those of social class structure and the diverse educative potential they imply. But what is missing from that conclusion, in terms of ethical theory, is any explicit consideration of the *kind* of equivalence or equality we should unqualifiedly approve of, and so seek to realize. As I have already remarked, there is an endless number of ways in which persons can be said to be equal or unequal. Each of these implies the specification of some domain of relationship with respect to which equality can be affirmed or denied. Otherwise the concept is meaningless. One is therefore seeking to define such a domain, in which equality would be attainable, and would have the highest ethical priority.

What comes first, in the explication I have to offer, is that equality depends on human individuality and thus also upon our *differences* from each other. If one tries to imagine a society of persons literally indistinguishable from each other, in the manner of sodium atoms, I think it is clear that its members would not have reason to value each other as equal individuals. Perhaps the grimmest version of this thought experiment is to imagine a society consisting entirely of duplicates of oneself. A second image, almost equally horrible, is that of a society in which one person is superior to *all* others in *every* conceivable respect, superior in the rather strong sense, that for this supreme or dominating individual there is literally nothing to be learned, nothing not already experienced or understood or mastered, through association with the lesser multitude.

In his zeal to describe an ideal embodiment of all the human virtues Aristotle in his *Ethics* came perilously close to this, his image of the "great-minded" man. By very definition this paragon had nothing to learn from the lives of others, nothing to emulate or be intrigued or challenged by. A canny philosophical critic could thus immediately create a logical paradox, pointing out that in claiming *all* excellence for the "great-minded" one Aristotle was inevitably extending the definition of virtues to include one which his hero lacked: the art of learning from others. It is in fact just that kind of virtue I have in mind as relevant to the root meaning of equality. We are valuable to each other in practicing and learning the art of living (and all the lesser arts and sciences) by the measure, and in the diversity, of our individual skills, talents, and achievements, actual or potential.

One side of this virtue is expressed in Kant's principle of obligation, that we should treat others as ends in themselves, never as means only. As we violate Kant's axiom we cut ourselves off, and those we treat as means only, from the human sources out of which the arts and sciences may be extended. Spinoza puts it differently, as a principle of utility, and draws my implication for me:

... there is nothing more profitable to man for the preservation of his being and the enjoyment of a rational life than a man who is guided by reason. Again, since there is no single thing we know which is more excellent than a man who is guided by reason, it follows that there is nothing by which a person can better show how much skill and talent he possesses than by so educating others that at last they will live under the direct authority of reason. (*Ethics*, Book IV, Appendix IX).

Neither Kant nor Spinoza makes the emphasis I want, however, upon the diversity and incommensurability of human talents and achievements. This, I hold, is the real root of the Kantian respect for autonomy *and* of the Spinozaistic enjoyment of its fruits.

Here I defer instead to John Stuart Mill, whose defense of liberty was to argue for the tolerance and support of divergent perspectives, persuasions, and commitments, because of the long-run value of that diversity to all the members of a society characterized by it.

Whatever the implications of genetic difference in our evolution, in the time scale of our more recent history its role is taken over decisively by our nongenetic, cultural variety and the individuality which only human careers can evolve. By the nature of the great brain's assimilation and endless recreation of culture our profiles of talent and of learning are jagged and uneven, and in this fact lies the analogue of complementary genetic variety, of the robustness our existence requires in the face of a changing world. Here as in biological evolution what counts is a richness of preadaptation, a variety which prepares us for an uncertain future. But of course mere diversity is not enough. What counts for robustness in the reproductive pool of culture is not random variety but the search for better modes of knowledge, of expression, of organization. This "better" entails a value judgment and a criterion. The criterion is supplied in its most adequate and briefest form by Spinoza's phrase, to "live under the direct authority of reason."

I don't propose to explicate fully a concept so enshrined in tradition as that of reason. What I wish to do rather is follow the suggestion of Spinoza's corollary, and go directly to the matter of education.

Reason in the way Spinoza uses the term is not a matter of mere logicality or orderliness, it is the capacity for finding and creating new order, for syntheses, for making ideas more adequate. In John Dewey's philosophy of experience the classical ideal of Reason is translated as the function of inquiry in the continuum of experience. It is the ability to find what is problematic and to guide inquiry toward "instituting a unified state of affairs" in knowledge, in skill or technique, in artistic expression, and finally also in the fashioning of coherent practical ends out of disparate and initially conflicting strands of need, interest, and knowledge. Dewey avoided the word "Reason" in the old eulogistic sense. It brought with it, he thought, a variety of dualisms, besetting sins of previous philosophy. Nevertheless, there has not been a philosopher more loyal to the tradition which the word connotes.

Such synoptic and unifying abilities, whether we call them Reason or Inquiry, are recognized by Dewey as individual capacities which we can develop through working association with others. Experience is not intrinsically private; it is, in fact, essentially social. The distinction between private and public, individual and social, is a distinction *within* experience, which marks phases in the constant transaction of collective existence.

The idea of equality, seen in such a context, implies equivalence across a domain of human interactions at this basic moral, intellectual, and esthetic level. What it means is that we do not *by nature* outrank each other uniformly around the profile of our talents and achievements. Rankings will indeed appear in this or that special context; some will be leaders and some followers, but by turns. Where global rankings appear, these must be regarded as symptomatic of institutional and cultural ill-health. Institutions which foster such social illness are to be challenged and, as we have knowledge and can define means, reformed.

If one wants to measure human abilities it is necessary that the logical structure of the measure should match that of the things measured. This means, as I have already suggested by the many-dimensional rosette profile, that the array of measures corresponding to those many dimensions is irreducible to any single aggregate measure except for special and merely local purposes. Any good measure of human abilities is a vector of many components, not a single scalar quantity permitting universal ranking.

But incommensurability is not equality; it is mathematically a weaker axiom. To get to the stronger form it is useful I think to bring back and underline, from the classical political documents, the concept discussed earlier, that of fraternity. What I mean is not a sentimental and uncritical avowal of fraternal love, but a context within which we can be equal, one in which we can all further educate one another "under the direct authority of reason." The criterion must be that of educative influence in all our dealings. In human affairs both large in scale and local, it means that everyone must have some voice. We should add this to life, liberty, and the pursuit of happiness as an inalienable right.

One has no voice if one is silenced or excluded, and that

was Mill's concern. But one also has no voice if one has nothing to say, or if the voice only plays back what the ear has recorded. This is where education comes into the argument, the effort to educe those kinds of learning which realize the promise of our potential value to each other. Education in this context is not limited to schooling. Indeed where schooling is restricted and narrow other educational influences may shine by comparison. Nate Shaw* was illiterate but, as one reviewer said, "illiterate like Homer."

The stronger form of the axiom of equality, that of equivalence or equality across the high-priority domain of transactions contributory to the good life of all, expresses a potentiality not to be established or disproved by limited stretches of experience, however disciplined by scientific rigor. It lies in the logical region of propositions which commit us rationally to important *directions* of work—not to final conclusions—which require us to keep open and explore possibilities beyond or in contravention of what is currently believed. Though such propositions cannot be established or disproved by limited collections of evidence they can be *con*firmed or *in*firmed, strengthened or weakened, by evidence, they are not pie in the sky. Decisions concerning them may hasten or long postpone the growth of knowledge. They represent scientific investment decisions made, as investments always are, in the presence of some uncertainty. My argument is for a certain kind of reinvestment in egalitarian aims, redefined and extended.

---

* Theodore Rosengarten, *All God's Dangers: The Life of Nate Shaw* (New York: Knopf, 1974).

When the first "weak" interactions in particle physics were carefully investigated, the results threatened to contradict that classical law of physics which had enjoyed almost axiomatic status, the conservation of energy and momentum. One might have decided that the law was down the drain, and indeed that possibility was much discussed. But then a new alternative was proposed, the neutrino, a massless particle which by its definition accounted for the missing energy and momentum. This particle had, at first sight, the convenient property of being undetectable, and that seemed to make it a too-easy way of saving a sacred principle. At the time, I heard the neutrino hypothesis attacked on that very ground: unverifiable. Then it turned out the neutrino was indeed detectable, though by nonstandard means. In the end the neutrino was detected by those means, and now enjoys the status of being a member, indeed a type, of the newfound tribe which high-energy particle physics must account for. But energy and momentum were saved.

It appears to me that the belief in human equality, formulated in terms of this world by the modern classical philosophers and hard won in the political struggles of their age, has undergone a similar crisis in the growth of late nineteenth-century genetics, which seemed to challenge these beliefs and to reinstate older, and still popular, beliefs in innate inequality. Even if, as I argued at the outset, this challenge was only at the level of a second approximation, the revisions or reversions it suggested had important negative implications for the ideals of universal education.

But with the further growth of genetics, with the newfound grasp of the role of genetic information in embryology, and with increased attention to the interactive character of child development and learning, we are in a position to introduce some neutrino-like novelty to perturb both the classical view *and* its outright denial. It is a move which rejects both Social Darwinism and Social Lysenkoism.

The standard hereditarian view leads logically to programs of stratified education, to Plato's picture of selective education predetermined with respect to status or class. The standard environmentalist view leads logically to programs that recognize no congenital diversity and recognize differences only as environmentally induced, as matters for "remediation." Such programs require but one uniform educational track which, apart from catching up the slow ones, provides "equality of opportunity." The first sort of program tends to be strongly self-confirming, the second to fail.

The novelty in the picture, I have urged, is the full conceptual accreditation of the importance of nature-nurture interaction in human development, along with the implied commitment to extend our knowledge of the kinds of complementary provisions for children's education which will move toward egalitarian goals. In accrediting such a conception one would of course share, with the "100 percent environmentalists," the commitment to try to eliminate early childhood environments, whether from poverty or the middle class, which are 100 percent narrowing or stultifying to children in general. But one would be especially concerned to find the less visible strengths of children who have already been damaged, for whatever reasons, congenital or otherwise. In such cases the exploration must be wide, and even partial success will be informative.

The neutrino was conjectural only for a few years and its promotion to the status of reality was the work of a few physicists costing, I suppose, a few million dollars. Our case is completely different in scale, in style, in tempo, in human importance. The evidence is more diffuse and there is more of it to start with, though mostly in the biographies of successful teachers. Single cases do not "prove" as though they were crucial experiments, but they can powerfully illuminate, if one looks well and does not resort to the handy basket called Miracle. The story of Helen Keller is a case in point, too often thrown into that basket if looked at at all. The only decisive evidence, however, will be cumulative success or failure.

I cannot try here to spell out what this perspective might imply for the reform of our institutions of early education.* The scale and magnitude of changes needed are great but not utopian. First and second steps have already been made in some places, reduced to successful practice. But the whole process is too complex for any single programmatic scheme of reform; it must be the product of an intelligent evolution and an informed vision of possibilities. Studies which demonstrate the inefficacy of our recent relatively large-scale efforts to improve education for the children of poverty are valuable for showing that many of the panaceas we have tried out so far have been at the wrong level, and

---

* I have tried in *The Informed Vision* (New York: Agathon Press, 1974).

on the wrong time scale, and to ends badly defined. Many of the changes needed are simply not of the kind which can be "designed," "installed," or "adopted" by congressional decision or administrative fiat. Needed and possible first steps there are, but these have far more the character of educational statesmanship, which we seem to lack, than of educational technocracy, which we have in abundance. The statesmanship I think of sees as fundamental a major direction of change and works, over time, to encourage and bring together the many strands of development necessary to progress in that direction.

But this theme also leads beyond my present purpose. For this purpose my argument is simply that human beings can, ideally, attain *equal* levels of educated talent, knowledge, and creativeness in any area of human endeavor. Special and gross disabilities aside, our genetic diversity manifests itself as generalized inequality across a wide range of abilities only if some are subject to kinds of nurture and educative influence which, for them, are inappropriate.

If native learning abilities and learning "styles" differ constitutionally at birth, the late-stage embryology of the nervous system may in turn be affected by the match or mismatch of early stimulation; the optimal direction of learning itself, at each subsequent stage, will depend on which strands of development are ready, as a result of early interaction, to be woven together to evolve still more complex levels of learning. Thus in some cases early speech development may bring a child to levels of communication with adults which open doors onto human affairs at an age when other abilities are still relatively unformed. Other children may instead commit themselves early to the refinement of esthetic or manipulatory abilities, their significant communication being limited for a longer time to nonverbal exchange with adults able to share those engrossments. Late-maturing abilities will develop in contexts quite different from the same abilities appearing earlier, and the resulting later-stage syntheses will differ correspondingly in quality and use. Certain overall patterns of development will be universal or almost so, but the variable fine structure of development will early prefigure the emergence of individuality. Early interests and commitments may "organize" other aspects of learning, just as in green plants the highest growing tip, the apical meristem, will organize growth in other branches. But from the first dividing cell the plant's growth instructions are both simple and innate. In human learning the corresponding kind of directive influence is more diverse and is assimilated all along the way from sources that are both internal *and* external. A developmental focus which has been dominant for a time may be seemingly laid aside while new capacities are being worked on. The early bent of the twig should very properly keep us guessing about the later inclination of the branch. If growth determines form, it perhaps does not do so twice in the same way.

Yet in all this developmental diversity there is a kind of stability. Not only are there general developmental stages of the sort that Piaget has brought to wide recognition, but there is (or can be) a certain uniformity of basic substantive attainments. There are no children, in the wide normal

range, who are not originally apt for mathematics or literature or politics or moral insight. Even with fortunate early
lives they will develop these talents unequally, however,
along different biographical pathways. Such inequalities
will appear even in the midst of abundant opportunities,
not by deprivation but by what we may as well call choice.
Yet interests which are strongly focused can be helped to
broaden, to include learning of many kinds previously by-
passed.

The stability which brings diverse individuals to a state
of shared knowledge and inquiry, shared engrossment and
enjoyment—equality—is least of all limited by genetics,
and most of all by the bonds of a very strong continuity in
the educational potential and practice of any given social
group or society. To increase this potential a society must
first of all have some of it (which it has) and then must
determine to use the potential it already has, to increase it.
Legislatures cannot decree this potential, nor can revolutions create it, discontinuous with the past. In criticizing
Descartes' philosophical game of wiping the slate of knowledge clean and starting all over again on firm foundations,
Spinoza replied that the only foundation of knowledge is
knowledge. We can make tools, he said, only by using the
tools we have already made. One might thus vainly argue
either that tools were impossible or that there had always
been tools. But in fact, he said, men first used the crude
tools which they found in nature, and with these they
shaped better tools. So likewise with knowledge.

And so with education. In Dewey's early youth the demand for universal public education took as its model insti-

tutions and forms of schooling which had evolved earlier around the needs of an elite which was already educated. Though there have been great efforts toward expansion, adaptation, and reform in the following century, the ideal of universal education has so far been realized very unequally indeed. It remains true that the most significant single correlate of educational success in our schools, or by any more adequate measure, is the educational background from which children come.

Today a not negligible proportion of children avoid school altogether, in spite of the legal compulsion of the statute books. For a majority the function of school attendance is more custodial than educative. The truth is, I believe, that the institution itself has not evolved, by the measure of need, very far beyond its earlier function of extending an education *already* well begun and well supported along the way. For children not fitting that presupposition, schooling is in most respects a high-probability failure. We have not dug very deep into the early origins of learning, or recognized the human and scientific importance of the study of individuality, its roots, and its branches. We have allowed our formal educational system to lose any real momentum of development, any sense that one of its prime purposes is to learn more about the art of teaching. We support instead a style of "educational research" separated from the working life of schools and mostly irrelevant to that life.

Under these circumstances, at a time when our widespread failure to educate well is becoming more and more conspicuous, it is acutely inappropriate to assume that the causes of this failure lie in the "disabilities" of children, rather than in the educational disabilities of our society and of our characteristic patterns of schooling. I am not here arguing that facts discovered in following this inappropriate assumption are to be disregarded. Indeed, they have a certain importance. Out of the whole debate over the inheritance of abilities one can filter out one useful conclusion, which is that superficial efforts directed to the "remediation" of children doomed otherwise to fail in our schools will not amount to much. Indeed, such efforts have typically been based on the *same* assumption, that it is the child rather than the school which must be changed. Much of our Project Head Start, in particular, was dominated by this way of thinking. Its aim was to create a new kind of "readiness," not readiness for learning important things at this or that level, but readiness for an uncriticized and unaltered future called *first grade*. Since the great majority of Head Start classes adopted the same format and style as the schools they were to ready children for, they were often in fact a head start to the failure they aimed to avoid.

This failure of most of our better-advertised efforts at remediation is of course grist for the mill of "hereditarian" thinking, according to which a sizable proportion of all, and an especially large proportion of black and other minority children, are doomed genetically to the failure they now experience in education and in later life. I have argued above that such thinking is based on inadequate scientific understanding. Here I wish to restate the case.

The potential talents and abilities of any newborn human being are wrongly expressed by the image of a fixed innate potential in this or that dimension, and by the mathematical counterpart of that image, a measure. That potential is correctly expressed for each individual not by a single measure, or three of four, but by a function, one depending both on genetic variables and on many environmental variables, each representing a whole history of nurtural and educative influence. The genetic or constitutional basis of individuality is expressed not by any measure but by the character and shape of this function, differing significantly from one child to the next. In particular, these innately different functions are such that a cohort of children who live under ideally identical circumstances will develop differently and in general unequally. Optimal or at least good environments for some types of children may be relatively abundant in some sectors of a society; for other types of children such environments may be rare overall, having thus no influence on population statistics. Such children are indeed doomed by that fact to low levels of talent and achievement.

But the whole picture is essentially more complicated than this. Even in principle, two different children cannot be subjected to the "same" environment. Like heredities, environments are reactive; they respond differently to different individuals. Environments cannot be properly conceived as fixed quantities, "stimuli" or the like. Environments respond as functions of the ways in which different children impinge upon them. In our world a black skin, or any other such mark of minority status undeniably genetic in origin, may notoriously stimulate an "environment" to give quite special responses which are far from optimal in an educational sense.

Such a general framework for the description of human learning and development is complex, but I believe it is irreducibly so. If so, there is no scientific virtue in regressing from it to simplistic views about the ways the human mind and character develop, or to the no longer tenable folklore of "inheritance." Science does in the end bring us to know what we can and cannot do, but considered as science, the belief in fixed hereditary potentialities is about on a plane with Aristotle's version of the laws of motion. Both generalize from a range of experience that is limited and uncontrolled. Rocks do fall and fire rises, while what is up above goes round in circles. The statistics are good but the thought habits which interpret them need reconstruction in the light of wider knowledge. As a result of that kind of reconstruction we know that a sow's ear *can* be turned into a silk purse (it is the reverse transformation which we must be more respectful about). What we do not yet know, at least in a coherent codified way, is how to organize our partial and uneven knowledge of learning and teaching to the end that all shall be well educated.

The ethics of education conspires, in this way, with the scientific need to redirect investigation to a deeper level than is expressed in the dominant practice of our institutions. A vital part of this practice must in the nature of the case be a serious and continuing investment in the kind of institution which Dewey created and studied, the experimental school. A much better part would be an infusion of that same investigative spirit, away if necessary from college campuses, into the common schools themselves. It would provide them where possible with the pragmatic best of the existing art of teaching, and with the kinds of thoughtful and widely informed research that are capable of supporting and benefiting from the art, interaction on still another level. Better practice can only grow organically and unevenly; it will not grow unless we work to create higher peaks of potential, reduced to practice. In our recently developed concern for the welfare of education we have supported some such efforts, but these efforts have themselves been generally regarded as "experiments" with some particular model or plan. The effort to infuse schools with an investigative spirit, to provide them with the material, intellectual, and moral support which such a spirit can thrive on, should not itself be thought of as an experiment, one which must justify its existence in the short run, as though what we already have is too good to be perturbed or jeopardized. The need to support such schools is not at issue; it should be acknowledged as policy, as dogma. Their accountability should be that of research institutes, not that of single experiments.

In such a style of development and research what counts as evidence concerning the educability of children from different backgrounds is success—success at levels improbable within our now existing educational systems. In that sort of "research design" failure counts as evidence only as it is analyzed and exploited for new designs; above all it is not evidence of impossibility, it is not imputed to children as a mark upon their foreheads. The limits of education, about which we know very little, are not to be defined by failure, but by success. Our knowledge of the impossibility of perpetual-motion machines has not been acquired through the repeated failure to make them, but from success in the creation and analysis of many *other* sorts of machines and from the general principles distilled from that success. The law of conservation of energy was first surmised from the boring of cannon, the second law from the study of the steam engine. The knowledge that perpetual motion is impossible comes only indirectly, from quite grand and final formulations.

The field of human learning is one very different from physics in style and tempo of development, and in the kinds of understanding which the subject matter allows. But the logic remains the same. We will not know what is impossible of achievement, except by the achievement of what is possible. And that effort is, in any case, a moral commitment.

INDEX

Index

Sherman, Gen. W. T., 37
Shockley, W., 64n
Skinner, 77
Smith, P. V., 64n
Smythies, J. R., 86n
Snow, R. E., 96n
Social contract, 22, 23–24, 25
Socialism, 22
Spencer, Herbert, 54
Spinoza, B., 3, 103, 104, 105, 113
Stanford-Binet test, 19
State of nature, 23, 25
Szillard, Leo, 57n

Talents: *see* abilities and talents
Teaching: art of, 7; research and experiments in, 114–15, 117–19

Test design, 75, 88–89, 91
Transmission: concept of, 77–78

Utility: as basis of equality, 103

Wallace, A. R., 29
Wallace, Bruce, 56n
War, 20, 23, 25
Winstanley, Gerrard, 26
WISC Wechsler Information Sub-test, 75
Wright, Sewell, 52